$15-

D0992372

THREE
INSTANCES
OF INJUSTICE

THREE
INSTANCES
OF INJUSTICE

K. R. Eissler

International Universities Press, Inc.
Madison   Connecticut

Copyright © 1993, International Universities Press, Inc.

All rights reserved. No part of this book may be reproduced by any means, nor translated into a machine language, without the written permission of the publisher.

Library of Congress Cataloging-in-Publication Data

Eissler, K. R. (Kurt Robert), 1908-
    Three instances of injustice / K.R. Eissler.
        p.   cm.
    Includes bibliographical references and index.
    ISBN 0-8236-6530-5
    1. Justice. 2. Morgan, Elizabeth, 1947-   —Trials, litigation,
etc. 3. Custody of children. 4. Freud, Sigmund, 1856-1939-
-Correspondence. 5. Jung, C.G. (Carl Gustav), 1875-1961-
-Correspondence. 6. Psychotherapist and patient. I. Title.
HM216.E36 1993
303.3'72—dc20   93-21078
                                                                             CIP

Manufactured in the United States of America

TABLE OF CONTENTS

Introduction   vii

Dr. Elizabeth Morgan's Contempt of Court
or, Justified Suspicion and Conclusive
Evidence of Sexual Abuse of Children   1
    Excursus on the Supreme Court,
    Abortion and the Death Penalty   50

C. G. Jung, a Witness
or, the Unreliability of Memories   107

The Maligned Therapist
or, an Unsolved Problem of Psychoanalytic
Technique   185

Epilogue   249

Acknowledgments   255

Name Index   257

Subject Index   261

INTRODUCTION

From its title the reader may be led to expect more than he will find in this book. He will rightly remark that the main topic of each essay is inconsequential and pale when held against the atrocious injustices that have occurred in our own as well as former times. Even the 759 days of imprisonment for civil contempt of court that Dr. Elizabeth Morgan suffered in the custody case of her daughter, the topic of the first essay, may not be considered grievous.

Still, the essays in this volume are not without some relevance to social concerns at the century's close. In pursuing the ramifications of the Morgan case, I felt it obligatory to reflect on the Supreme Court and its appalling callousness vis-à-vis capital punishment. The barbarism of death row, where 2,200 people are kept under inhuman conditions waiting to be executed, is a truly shocking matter, a canker on our society, which condones the practice. Capital punishment and death row are moral disasters for which the whole community carries responsibility and is dishonored by guilt: a defilement beyond words.

The second and third essays inhabit a more peaceful climate. In the former I disclose as a falsification testimony which years ago was believed to expose the moral corruption of a noted scholar and was cited all over the world. In the latter I examine the transitory disarrangements two scholars brought into my psychoanalytic practice by publishing unbridled confabulations about me.

Thus, only the excursus on the Supreme Court may transmit the feeling that I am touching upon a nerve center. Even this contribution cannot be called original, for others have raised similar criticisms; possibly I do it with a nuance more passion and vehemence than is usual. I am certain that my suggestion of how to redress and put the situation to rights is original; I am as certain that it will be rejected as outlandish, to say the least, and ridiculed as impracticable. Nevertheless, it may not have been futile to bring it up.

I should have liked to advance ideas about the definition and theory of justice and injustice, but I am in no position to add to the debates carried on by philosophers and moralists. I expect that whenever I use the terms, the readers will have no difficulty in understanding in what sense they are used.

Dr. Elizabeth Morgan's Contempt of Court or, Justified Suspicion and Conclusive Evidence of Sexual Abuse of Children[1]

Dr. Elizabeth Morgan, a prominent plastic surgeon, spent 759 days in the Washington, D.C., Detention Center, by reason of civil contempt. This was longer than anyone has ever been held without a foregoing trial and conviction, merely following a closed-court proceeding, except for some reputed mobsters who refused to betray their partners in crime.

Morgan was certain that her former husband, Dr. Eric Foretich, an oral surgeon, had sexually abused their daughter, Hilary. Having failed to persuade the court to end unsupervised visitation with the father, she sent her daughter into hiding and refused to reveal her whereabouts. This act prompted Judge Herbert B. Dixon, Jr. of the District of Columbia Superior Court to charge her with contempt of court and order

[1]All facts directly referring to the Morgan-Foretich custody case are taken from the magazine articles listed in the References, unless otherwise stated. I am deeply indebted to the authors for their excellent reporting, which made this essay possible.

1

her incarceration. To many people she became a symbol of true motherhood, for in her determination to protect her child from what appeared to her an abusive, destructive father and a callous, indifferent court, she was ready to stay in jail until her daughter would come of age, in the year 2000. For some time the case was a national cause and was taken up by feminist groups and columnists; a group named the Friends of Elizabeth Morgan sent out news releases and picketed the Washington, D.C. District Court every Wednesday throughout the period of Morgan's incarceration.

The Morgan-Foretich case is highly unusual. It is the longest-running domestic suit in the District of Columbia's history, involving 75 witnesses, more than 500 pleadings, more than 4,000 pages of transcripts and several million dollars in legal fees; but as far as the custody litigation as such is concerned, it shares its basic structure with hundreds, if not thousands, of similar cases. To go into its details may nevertheless be worthwhile, because they raise a number of challenging issues as well as a puzzling problem, to be brought up at the end of my remarks, that no one seems to have noticed. I shall first introduce superficial profiles of the protagonists.

Dr. Eric A. Foretich, born in 1943, the son of an electrical engineer, had enjoyed an idyllic childhood of fishing trips and sand-lot baseball in Virginia when at age 16 he was severely traumatized by the death of his one-month-old baby sister following a blood transfusion. Soon afterward he decided to attend the College of William and Mary, where in 1965 he met the schoolteacher who was to become his first wife. He suffered a new personal loss in 1968 when his younger brother was killed in a car accident at age 21. In 1969, at a time when he was taking his internship and residency in New York, his wife filed for divorce on grounds of desertion. He returned to Virginia in 1972 and started a successful practice, earning $175,000 a year. He was fully engaged in his work until 1977 when, after a one-year courtship, he married a stunning 20-year-old model. In 1978 his first child was stillborn. In 1980 the couple had a daughter, Jane, but the marriage did not work out. When he met Morgan in 1981, his second marriage was already on the brink. Dr. Foretich was a Catholic who became a reborn Christian.

Dr. Elizabeth Morgan was born in 1948. She grew up in an affluent Virginia suburb of Washington, D.C., as the daughter of two psychologists, who were divorced. She excelled from the start, skipped kindergarten and third grade, graduated within the top 10 percent of her high-school class, and entered Harvard at 16. She holds degrees from Radcliffe and Yale Medical School (1971) and studied at Oxford, England. After completing a seven-year residency she established herself as one of Washington's preeminent plastic surgeons and earned $400,000 the year before she was jailed. She was the medical columnist for *Cosmopolitan* magazine and is the celebrated author of four books, including the bestseller *The Making of a Woman Surgeon*. After so many years of hard work she was ready for romance when in the fall of 1981 she met Foretich, a good-looking man with a shock of unruly hair. Oddly enough, it had been Sharon, Foretich's second wife, who, after having seen Morgan on the Donahue show discussing her bestseller, called her husband's attention to her, since he was looking for a plastic surgeon to whom to refer patients.

Both Morgan and Foretich were on the staff of Fairfax Hospital in Virginia. The purpose of their first meeting was business, but she was deeply touched by his story, his unhappiness in facing a second divorce. A whirlwind courtship followed: walks in the park, elegant dinners, evenings at the ballet. She was madly in love with him when she became pregnant. In January 1982 they flew to Haiti, where Foretich, since he was only separated from Sharon, obtained a divorce—which, as it turned out later, was not valid. Morgan and Foretich were married in Haiti. Soon troubles arose. Morgan's aging, divorced mother joined them, and Foretich's irascible temperament became manifest. He had fits of rage when the two women occasionally shared confidences behind locked doors. He threw tantrums at the slightest provocation and accused Morgan of ruining his life. Violent incidents came to pass.

He had not told Sharon of their divorce and his remarriage. When this was announced in a gossip column of the *Washington Post*, he is said to have flown into such a rage that he knocked Morgan down and kicked her. However, he denies this and refuses to acknowledge his temper tantrums in general, but a witness confirmed that when Sharon gave birth to a baby girl, he was enraged that it was not a boy and acted so wildly in the delivery room that he had to be forced to leave the hospital. Morgan said her initial feelings, to which she should have paid heed, were that Foretich was a "jerk," a "bit of a come-on." He did impress her as clever, attractive and full of energy, but, according to her, he is an intelligent, educated, dangerous psychopath. Foretich's reaction to

Morgan, in turn, is that she was articulate and smart, but a very sick woman whom he married only because she was pregnant. It was noble of him to want to give the baby his name, but in the long run it would have been better if he had not done it.

Morgan decided to stay with her husband even after he had knocked her about. She was unaware that Foretich was calling Sharon daily (as she later deposed), professing his love to her and questioning whether the child Morgan was carrying was his. Foretich suffered from a distressing obsessive symptom. All during Morgan's pregnancy he kept saying over and over again that the baby would die, that he was miserable and nothing could cheer him up. Sharon states that he made the same morbid prediction when she was pregnant the first time. Being sure of the baby's death, he warned her against taking a shower. In that instance the prediction came true when Foretich's first baby was, as noted, stillborn. He held Sharon responsible and was constantly critical and angry, as he was later with Morgan. When he repeatedly threatened to kill both Sharon and himself, she finally left him.

One week before Hilary's birth, in August 1982, when Morgan was in false labor, she left Foretich, but later informed him that the birth was imminent and that tests had shown it was a girl. This time he allegedly said it would be better if the baby were dead. Morgan saw him the day after delivery. He pleaded for reconciliation, claiming to be the unhappiest man in the world. He did not look at the infant. Their marriage continued to decline, and five months later Morgan obtained a divorce in Haiti. When Hilary was nine months old, Morgan sued for child support and

Foretich countersued for custody, but he was granted only visitation rights. He visited the infant several times a week at the home of her baby sitter. He then petitioned the Court for the right to overnight visits, which began in June 1983. In November 1984 Morgan was awarded sole custody.[2]

I shall now turn to Hilary's story, which will give occasion for further comments on her parents. Hilary's symptoms started at the age of nine months. She would scream for no ostensible reason and have violent nightmares. What Morgan called Hilary's hysterical behavior started in June 1983 when the child began to spend alternate weekends with her father. The bouts of screaming almost always set in after she returned home from overnight visits; on one occasion she cried for 12 hours straight. The child's negative responses to the visits worsened and she would fall to the floor and scream until she was hoarse. Because of her violent nightmares Hilary was never able to sleep in the dark again, and from then on the mother had to rock her daughter to sleep. Sharon had told Morgan that her daughter, Jane, then three years old, showed symptoms after weekend visits with her father, threw tantrums and complained that her bottom hurt. She spoke vividly of taking baths with her father and playing with his penis. Morgan, in her naiveté, as she calls it, was convinced that, weird as she believed Foretich to be, he would never do anything to hurt his children. In retrospect she thinks she should have wondered about her daughter's inconsolable screaming fits. To her horror, one morning in January 1985,

---

[2]The time sequences one culls from the various articles are in some instances contradictory, which does not, however, obscure the general trend of events.

Hilary, then two-and-a-half years old, suddenly proceeded to describe, in unmistakable terms, oral sex with her father. She also would open her mouth and stick out her tongue when she was kissed goodnight and once picked up a banana and rubbed it between her legs, making panting noises. Every day Hilary would provide new revelations and would give similar reports to her nanny, who had been wondering for a time why her attempts to wash the little girl's genital area evoked hysteria. At last the mother thought she understood Hilary's neurotic symptoms, for which she had gone to several physicians, none of whom had brought relief.

Morgan decided not to confront Foretich, anticipating denial and rage. She was determined to suppress her own, to keep calm and to proceed in a rational manner. She consulted Dr. Joseph Noshpitz, a child psychiatrist affiliated with Children's Hospital in Washington, D.C., who reported her suspicion to the Department of Social Services in Fairfax County. There, Daisy Morrison-Gilstrap, a social worker, started interviewing Hilary on February 15, 1985, and concluded from her play-acting with dolls that the child had been sexually abused, the identity of the perpetrator unknown.

At that point there occurred one of those bizarre incidents of which this story is so full. Hilary's paternal grandfather was so incensed by the social worker's findings, which incriminated his son, that, in order to clear his son's name, he proposed the examination of his older granddaughter, Jane, then five years old. Morrison-Gilstrap complied, and her findings were reviewed by a county social services panel, which concluded that there was reason to suspect abuse in both girls. Jane described her own experiences with her father and confided that "Daddy hurts Hilary" in the same way. Sharon immediately resorted to action. Her lawyer, unable to prove abuse by Foretich, swayed the Fairfax County Court to rule that the decision on overnight visits should be left to the therapist. Since Jane felt intensely frightened by her father, it was decided that she should not visit him under any circumstances. Foretich opposed that decision and urged the Court to appoint other psychologists. Four times the Court complied with his request, but each subsequent psychologist opposed the grant of visitation rights to the father. Once, Foretich was permitted to meet Jane in the psychologist's office; the girl repeated her former denunciation in his presence and maintained that she did not want to visit with him. Foretich has not seen his older daughter for several years. In 1989 Sharon filed a claim against him seeking compensatory and punitive damages for his actions toward her and her daughter.

Hilary's case proved more complicated. She was too young to be a creditable witness, but Morgan was sure she would obtain a favorable ruling from Judge Dixon, in view of the identical physical findings in Jane. After all, when two girls, daughters of two mothers living at some distance from each other, accused the father of sexual abuse, this would amount to a smoking gun. But Judge Dixon decided that any information regarding Hilary's sister was irrelevant and therefore inadmissible. He granted the father unsupervised visitation in July 1986.

I have to interrupt my account of the sequence of events here and report a bizarre incident that made

Morgan appear in a dubious light and was used by Foretich to reduce her credibility. Morgan had taken pictures of Hilary inserting crayons and demitasse spoons into her vagina, which is said to be a typical reenactment by a child who had been sexually abused. According to the mother, she had been advised by a police officer to take the pictures for the purpose of gathering additional evidence of the infant's disturbed behavior. As a plastic surgeon she repeatedly had to take shocking and graphic photographs for purposes of evidence. The film processors spotted the negatives and informed Morgan that they either had to destroy them or turn them over to the authorities as being pornographic. Morgan had them sent to the Department of Social Services, to be seen by Morrison-Gilstrap. Later, after Morrison-Gilstrap had left her position, they were forwarded, by an unknown source, to the Washington, D.C. Police Department. The police officer who allegedly had advised Morgan about the photographs denied having done so, and for two years a criminal investigation was conducted against her on charges of pornography; the charges were eventually dropped by the Department of Justice as well as the U.S. Attorney's Office because there was no criminal intent on the mother's side. But Foretich saw them as "a stunning indictment of Morgan" and proof that she was a "pervert."

Morgan decided to defy Judge Dixon's visitation orders of July 1986 and was, therefore, jailed twice for a period of three days each. But she succeeded in keeping Hilary from her father for the rest of the year, and the girl's state changed markedly for the better.

In order to evade Judge Dixon's insistence on unsupervised visitation, Morgan's attorneys worked out a new strategy. The plan was to bring the case before a jury—Judge Dixon had heretofore opposed a trial by jury. The attorneys were certain that, if the facts were heard by 12 average people, and not just one judge, the verdict would be favorable. A suit was filed in a federal court in Virginia against Foretich and his parents for damages caused by sexual abuse. Foretich countersued for defamation of character. Both sides lost, and both sides appealed. Again, only part of the evidence reached the jury. U.S. District Court Judge Richard Williams excluded all information about Jane as well as all findings by the child therapist, psychologist, and social worker. Even a videotape of Hilary's statements to various professionals was ruled inadmissible as hearsay evidence. In addition, the procedure was confusing to the jury because of conflicting testimony by experts, which will be discussed later.

The loss of the federal case had the consequence that in April 1987 Hilary saw her father again in unsupervised weekend visits. Hilary's condition, which had improved so conspicuously, worsened alarmingly. Two psychiatrists diagnosed a multiple personality disorder; she became suicidal; and her descriptions of what happened during visitations became intolerable in their graphic obviousness. Mother and therapist requested that officials of the Court social services resume the investigation, but no reply was received: the Department was incapable of handling its massive case load. Morgan's pleas for police help were likewise futile. Furthermore, all files concerning Foretich's daughters were destroyed at the order of the Virginia Social Services Commissioner, in response to an appeal by Foretich's attorney.

Then, in August 1987, there happened what Morgan considered the last straw. Judge Dixon declared the evidence in equipoise, meaning that both the probability and the improbability of Hilary's having been raped by her father were equal; this meant to him that there was no conclusive evidence of abuse, and he ordered unsupervised visitation for two weeks, beginning with Hilary's fifth birthday. Morgan, in consultation with Hilary's psychotherapist, decided that her daughter should go into hiding. One morning in August 1987 Morgan drove her daughter to a diner on a highway in Virginia where another car was waiting, and the period of Hilary's covert existence began. Her grandparents, William Morgan, 79, and Antonia, 74, who had reconciled, took the child under their care.

In order not to leave too abysmal an impression about the unwisdom of judicial institutions, I quote here a Court opinion that is more in keeping with the common sense of laymen. While Hilary was in hiding and Morgan in jail, the U.S. Fourth Circuit Court of Appeals, after reviewing the evidence that Morgan had presented and that which had been excluded by Judge Richard Williams, decided on May 17, 1988, that there was sufficient evidence to justify a finding of sexual abuse and, further, that the evidence pertaining to Jane was relevant, since it identified Foretich as the perpetrator. Only he had access to both girls. Nothing else could have been equally probative. Therefore, the Court decided that Foretich's explanations were not credible. The father's defenses of self-infliction and fabrication by Hilary or abuse by the mother became implausible. Hilary's statements to her mother and to the experts should have been admitted as evidence. This decision by the Court of Appeals, however, came too late, since, as mentioned, the child was already in hiding and the mother in jail.

At this point I shall present, in the form of an abbreviated survey, the rich harvest of expert opinions that had accumulated. There is objective evidence that Hilary was abused. Dr. Charles Shubin of Baltimore Mercy Hospital, an authority on the physical signs of molestation, found identical vaginal scarring and abnormal hymenal openings in Hilary and Jane. The sisters were examined three months apart and the pediatrician was ignorant of their parentage. The damage was caused by the insertion of an object, such as an erect adult penis, to a depth of about 1½ inches.

However, this testimony was partly contradicted by Dr. Catherine de Angelis, pediatrician at Johns Hopkins, called by Foretich to testify. In her opinion the enlargement of the opening could have been brought about by the objects that were shown on the aforementioned photographs that Morgan had taken while Hilary was masturbating. This opinion, in turn, was rejected by Shubin on two grounds: objects like crayons could not cause the enlargements of 10 millimeters that Hilary had; and such enlargements are too painful to be self-inflicted.

Dr. Dennis Harrison, a psychologist/child-abuse specialist who interviewed Hilary and reviewed the accumulated material, asserted that Hilary was the victim of severe continuing sexual abuse by penetration, that she consistently named her father as the culprit, and that her emotions were so powerful and spontaneous as to exclude coaching or rehearsal. In one session she became so upset when describing an incident that she inadvertently had a bowel movement.

Dr. David Corvin of the Oakland, California, Children's Hospital, a psychiatrist and pioneer in diagnostic techniques for determining sexual abuse of children, spent over 200 hours on Hilary. He concluded that she had been sexually molested and suffered from post-traumatic stress disorder. In his opinion, her descriptions of her experiences were far too detailed and emotionally charged to have been fabricated.

Dr. Mary Froning, a staff psychologist at the Chesapeake Institute of Maryland, a center for the study and treatment of sexually abused children and sex offenders, had extensive contact with Hilary. Initially the child was so frightened that Froning did not dare to voice a conclusive judgment. At that time Hilary already matched 13 out of 17 behavioral indicators of abuse. After three months Froning was convinced that the child had been severely abused and that the father was the perpetrator. It was one of the clearest among the more than 100 cases she had explored in her practice.

Hilary was seen 87 times by Froning. In session no. 9 Hilary said, "Daddy spanked me with his fucker," and pointed to her own vaginal area and that of the doll with which she was play-acting, to show where Daddy had spanked her. As time went on, a worsening picture of emotional abuse emerged. Her father, she reported, dangled her over a stove to scare her; he would kill mother and grandmother if she ever told.

Barbara C. Rollinson, the founder of the Metropolitan Methodist Nursery School in Washington, D.C., which Hilary attended from age two until she disappeared three years later, characterized her as "a live wire, popular and happy" at the beginning. About their last meeting, she related that she had "never seen a child so clinically depressed, like an adult. She was so tired she could not move. It was horrible." On another occasion she confirmed "that the child dramatically changed from the time the court ordered visitation until August, when Hilary left."

During the period of unsupervised visitation, when Hilary met her father she did not want to be a girl because it was too scary to be a girl, and she identified with her father in her play-acting and the girls were regularly the victims; after a period of not being in contact with him, she wanted to be a girl again, to wear pretty dresses and let her mother comb her hair. Before going into hiding, a multiple personality disorder developed; in the course of an hour, three selves would follow one another: the enraged girl that tried to hit and kick; the terrified girl; and the sweet, cuddly girl that would crawl into the therapist's lap. Frank Putnam, chief of the Unit on Dissociative Disorders at the National Institute of Mental Health, reviewed a 40-minute videotape of Hilary taken after her return from a weekend stay with her father and found the kind of personality split that occurs in children who have been exposed to repetitive abuse.

Hilary's behavior toward her playmates deteriorated. She would hit a playmate and turn around and say, "A friend has hit me." She acted out masochistic fantasies at home by pretending to shoot herself between the legs and saying, "My insides are all blood."

Then suicidal thoughts emerged. Once she picked up a butcher knife and talked about "sawing" herself so she would be dead. At another time she stood at the top of a flight of stairs and asked whether she would die and not see her father again if she threw herself down. She asked her mother to open a bottle of pills so that she could take them and die.

Another witness, Phyllis Savage, a probation officer, agreed to drive Hilary to visits with Foretich, but after one trip she refused to repeat it, for the girl's distress was so extreme that she screamed and cried uncontrollably throughout the trip.

In July 1986 Judge Dixon appointed Linda Holman *ad litem*—that is, to represent the child for the duration of the court suit. During the spring and summer of 1987 Holman petitioned the court ten times not to allow unsupervised visitation; Judge Dixon denied the motion ten times. Holman was in clear disagreement with Judge Dixon's order for the extended summer visitation; nevertheless, she stated, she could not argue that the order was without evidence to support it or that it was an abuse of the judge's discretion. Holman's behavior seemed contradictory and was never clarified. Judge Dixon allegedly had given her the power to stop any visit she deemed harmful to Hilary. Yet she sought an emergency stay of one such visit, maintaining that, if not Hilary's physical well-being, most assuredly her mental and emotional health were now in jeopardy. She, too, after two hideously anguished trips, refused to drive the girl to her father. But according to another version she took her there for unsupervised visits, checking on father and daughter for only one or two hours during each visit.

On one occasion, when the Judge had ordered a longer visit, Foretich and his parents came to pick her up. But the girl was so agitated and pleaded so much not to have to go that Morgan and her father, who was present, asked the Foretiches to leave, an action that Judge Dixon decreed to be in contempt of court and Morgan had to go to jail for a short time.

Of decisive weight, so one would think, should have been Sam Williams's testimony. He was a police detective with twenty years of service and a six-year specialization in child abuse. He was called in by two pediatricians of the Georgetown Hospital, where Morgan had taken Hilary. Upon her return from a visit with her father, she had told her mother that she had been raped vaginally and strangled. At the hospital it was confirmed that her vagina was inflamed. Even a veteran like Williams became upset, as he confessed after the interview with Hilary, by the description of her abuse; it brought tears to his eyes and hit him in the gut.[3]

By mid-July 1987 Froning got so alarmed about Hilary's condition that she risked a letter to Morgan advising her to stop the visits, whatever the legal consequences would be. According to her, Hilary had reached a point of greater hopelessness and depression than ever. The pressure that was put on her to submit to the visits made her sense that her feelings remained invalidated. If the meetings with her father had to continue, this would mean to her that her terror was inconsequential to her proximate environment, and that she was worthless.

---

[3]For unknown reasons his superiors, contrary to Williams's recommendation, closed any further investigation. Judge Dixon refused to hear Williams's testimony.

Against this formidable army of highly compromising informants, Foretich could raise only a platoon. His case relied primarily on the testimony of his fourth wife—he had married again after his divorce from Morgan but was separated from this new spouse at the time of the trial—his parents and nine friends, who said that Hilary was happy when they saw her at his home. Nor did all experts agree. Dr. Joseph Noshpitz was of the opinion that Hilary was a troubled child but that her symptoms were the result of tension between the parents. However, in his interview with the child he did not bring up the question of sexual abuse, nor did he use anatomical dolls, implements that are part of the standard procedure in the exploration of child abuse cases. More relevant seems to be the opinion of another psychiatrist, who contended that the three-year-old girl had abnormal sexual interests and tried to unbutton his fly. Dr. Elissa P. Benedek, professor of psychiatry at the University of Michigan Medical Center and president of the American Psychiatric Association, who testified on behalf of Foretich in the Virginia trial, said in a deposition, "I do not find any . . . convincing psychological evidence that Hilary Foretich has been sexually abused. . . . Hilary over time has been conditioned to make those statements and rewarded for that kind of behavior." Dr. Benedek's testimony will be discussed later, in conjunction with other statements she is alleged to have made. Finally, Arthur Green, a psychiatrist who had not met Hilary or read the reports, presented abstract discussions on the possibility of false allegations in child abuse cases.

Experts were also asked to evaluate the parents' personalities. Oddly enough, two psychologists whom Foretich had called upon to do a profile on him gave damaging evidence. Nancy Fretta found him to suffer from a narcissistic personality disorder; and according to William Zuckerman he had difficulty with boundaries, confusing his mother, his wives, and perhaps his daughters as objects of sexual need; aggressive impulses as well as sexual actions were not always within his control.

Here I want to include an impression Morrison-Gilstrap, who interviewed Foretich, recorded: he seemed less interested in the problem whose discussion was the purpose of their meeting than preoccupied with anger at his wives, in particular at Morgan and her success. He had a low opinion of women. He believed the male should be the dominant person in relationships, and it was not easy for him to accept his former wives' independence.

David Corvin interviewed both parents and found that custody should remain with the primary psychological parent, who in this case was Morgan. Hilary loved her mother very much, he maintained, and had been closely attached to her, and Morgan had been a conscientious and caring parent, while he found the father to have many of the traits typical of incestuous abusers. Dr. Carol Kleinman, Morgan's psychotherapist of long duration, publicly gave Morgan a clean bill of health. This, too, will be a topic for later discussion.

Indeed, in whatever direction one looks, something grating, to say the least, is encountered regarding Foretich, and one cannot help but take cognizance of what seems to amount to incontrovertible evidence of misdeeds on his part. It must have struck him like a nightmare in which he was the center of a conspiracy:

each of two daughters, their mothers, a federal appellate court, pediatricians, psychiatrists, psychologists, social workers, hospital employees, a police detective, everyone agreed he behaved in an unconscionable way. And what has Foretich to say under the impact of all these imputations of wrong-doing? He thrusts an adamant "No" at his accusers, promulgates his innocence and claims entrapment: it is a plot concocted by two of his ex-wives and the therapists paid by Morgan; Hilary loved him and Morgan felt threatened and wanted the child for herself; Morgan has coached Hilary; she is a sick woman and some people believe she is possessed; she has the coldest eyes he has ever seen; she is not a natural mother; she wants to be a physician, an author and, more important, a Joan of Arc; he prays every night for Hilary and for Elizabeth.

No doubt Foretich is a highly problematic personality of considerable psychological interest. Even under optimal conditions of exploration—let alone when only morsels scattered in magazines are known—it would be a hard task to grasp what is hidden behind his seemingly dualistic character: on the one hand, a most attractive and charming appearance and behavior combined with professional excellence, and, on the other hand, a comportment that often is provocative and even repugnant. At the center of his conflicts stand women. Evidently he is in great need of them and evidently he becomes easily irritated by them. He expects from them complete surrender; deviations from his expectations precipitate rage. His fear of them must be considerable. I surmise that he feels very affectionate toward them but judges his needs and affection to be weaknesses that have to be hidden behind an emphasis on male superiority and pride in his own gender. The fact of Foretich's four unsuccessful marriages evidences his inability to live alone as well as with a spouse. Yet the necessity of closeness to a woman makes him vulnerable, as observed in his inability to tolerate the intimacy between his wife and mother-in-law when they were living together. On the other hand, one wonders that a woman of such superior intelligence as Morgan refused to acknowledge how readily her husband's sense of security could be threatened.

To be sure, it is not easy for women to get along with males of that type, for such men have contradictory demands. They require females whose personalities or appearances flatter their self-esteem: women who in one way or another are superior. But there exists the danger that this superiority rebounds and overshadows that of their spouses', whose narcissism is thereby put in jeopardy. Then these men have to vilify their mates, in order to counteract the reduction in self-esteem. The extent of Foretich's vulnerability and the demands he puts on the female are illustrated in his rage at his wives for producing "only" girls as viable offspring; this affront becomes a matter of personal shame for the husband and is interpreted by him as a curse that the spouse's ill will casts on his existence.

In all that, Foretich's traumatization at age 16, when the newborn sister died, must not be forgotten. As mentioned before, he suffered from the compulsion to predict the deaths of the fetuses being carried by two of his wives. Possibly these obsessive thoughts were associated with the loss of his little sister during his boyhood. It may have had a devastating effect on the adolescent. Whether this was due to the activation of an unconscious memory of an earlier trauma, or one of those instances of a traumatic loss during adolescence that is followed by shattering effects from which the afflicted never fully recovers, cannot be decided. Foretich may unconsciously be looking for the lost infant whose death he had to witness. The desire to find the lost sister and the fear of losing her again would account for the observed ambivalence. In addition, the widespread magical practice of averting the occurrence of a dreaded event by predicting it was possibly operative at the same time.

It would be highly interesting if it turned out that those who, despite crushing evidence to the contrary, are convinced of Foretich's innocence were proved right. Then one would have to solve the puzzle of how an innocent person can get himself into such a network of circumstances that he appears almost irrefutably guilty. Victimology solves such surprising complications of life. In Foretich, traces of self-caused victimization can be discovered. The reader should be reminded of an incident presented earlier, even if it sounds far-fetched. Foretich's father requested an examination of his elder grandchild—something that could not have been done without Foretich's consent—and, promptly, in the light of its result Foretich's guilt loomed larger than ever. Likewise, he demanded a self-evaluation from a psychologist, and the result led to a grave self-indictment. He gives a pitiable list of the malignant sufferings he has been exposed to in the course of the custody fight, from his reduced practice to the disappearance of his child; yet all this he could have spared himself if he had not insisted on unsupervised visitation. His defense sounds at times childish and vindictive. He accuses Morgan of Hilary's sexual abuse but does not explain how it happened that his eldest daughter showed the same incriminating signs. He calls the examining physician incompetent without offering proof. The more active he is in his defense, the deeper he gets into trouble. An unconscious wish for punishment is prompted by actual misdeeds as well as forbidden desires. He would thus be a victim of what is inexactly named unconscious feelings of guilt, the rock on which so many falter. If he had kept quiet and done nothing but agree to supervised visitation of Hilary, he would not have had to face the many pitiable situations to which he was exposed following his refusal to accept a limitation on his visitation rights.

Foretich's several marriages would bespeak, among other shortcomings, a failure in making the right choices. Certainly, he should not have married Morgan, whose superiority to him in intelligence, efficiency and success could well have been a constant irritant. His rages, his impulsiveness, his penchant for irritating others, his inability to delay action, his low frustration level—all these conjoin to make him a tragic and deeply unhappy man in any case, whether he is innocent or guilty.

With Dr. Elizabeth Morgan one enters a different continent. Tragedy was not alien to her life, but she is endowed with a magnificent temperament that converts ordeals unbearable to others into unusual victories. Scholarly and professionally in the fore-front, she had a more than comfortable, exciting, and rewarding existence, but it was transformed from one moment to another into a hellish one, limited to a lightless 6-by-11-foot cell, an environment she had to share with prostitutes, addicts, and murderers. Like them, she was shackled and handcuffed on her frequent trips to court. The jail was always cold, and she developed tendinitis, a threat to her surgical skills. During the winter, prisoners were not allowed outside. They were awakened at 5 A.M.; lights and noise died down at 2 A.M. Her teeth loosened because of poor diet, and she suffered from chronic exhaustion. But all this did not sway her for a moment to shorten that wretched kind of existence, even though one word from her would have ended it.

She worked in the prison library, wrote a manual for women inmates, answered the numerous letters she received, and read voraciously—medical books and thick tomes she never had the time to read outside. She had her own technique of keeping up her morale. She did not count on being released on this or that date but looked at her state as a chronic one, not given to change. Judge Dixon said that the key to freedom was in her own hands. Her lawyers objected that incarceration for civil contempt was no longer coercion but punishment when it covered such an extensive period. The judge replied, "Coercion has only begun," but Morgan immunized that threat by her determination to stay in jail until the year 2000, when Hilary would be of age and could not be ordered to be with her father. (Her philosophy is superb.) She is said to have declared: "Whenever I feel sorry for myself, I remind myself we're not on this earth to have a good time. Nobody has got a contract to be happy, nor any reason to have been visited with as much undeserved misery as the absent Hilary." No doubt these are rational statements no one can gainsay; the marvel is that rationality affected her so deeply as to make her bear agony without complaint.

Dr. Foretich and his lawyers have a highly different view; they draw the picture of a narcissistic character for whom success is the highest value, a person who goes to prison in order to write a book and make a movie, all of which are closer to her heart, they claim, than being with her daughter. After all, what mother would bear separation from her child and let her go underground, without any chance of seeing her? Foretich speaks of her Joan of Arc complex. It is an intriguing question: was Joan of Arc, apart from her patriotic heroism, an exhibitionist? Here I want to interject only briefly—I will come back to it later—that Morgan acted under duress and had no choice but to send Hilary away, after Froning's clinical prediction of the child's suicide if she had to stay with her father one more time. Morgan's passport was taken from her, so she could not take flight abroad; her profile was, as she rightly said, too well-known in the United States for her to stay undercover for any appreciable time. From her point of view she had only the choice between contempt of court and her child's perdition.

There are those who try to escape the most distressing implications of Morgan's stay in jail by declaring her to be "crazy." In actions that deviate from common sense, the effect of some form of psychopathology is quickly detected. Her psychotherapist, however, excluded that eventuality. Morgan seems to be one of those rare people who are indefatigable and unyielding and remain undefeated even under the greatest stresses.

As often happens to select personages, fate was on her side. What appeared for a long time to be an abysmal and hopeless tragedy took, against all expectations, a lucky turn. In late September 1989, under intense national pressure, Congress passed a bill limiting, in the District of Columbia, incarceration for contempt of court to 12 months in cases of child custody. The bill was signed by the President on September 23, 1989, and Morgan was released two days later. Who would have thought it possible that the U.S. Congress would come to her help and Judge Dixon would be forced to dance to her tune and terminate the coercion shortly after he had boasted that it had just begun? It sounded just as improbable as the idea that she was capable of going through 759 days of imprisonment without a whine or whimper, but with the facility and sure-footedness we are accustomed to admire in a tightrope walker.

I have to add at last the bits and pieces I culled from various sources about the fourth voice in this woeful quartet: Judge Herbert B. Dixon. He was born in 1946. After graduating from Howard University and Georgetown University Law School, he clerked for Judge Carl Moultrie of the Superior Court in Washington, D.C. He formed his own general-practice law firm and often acted, at the court's request, as defense counsel in the Superior Court. He was appointed to the Washington, D.C. Superior Court by President Reagan at the recommendation of the local political establishment. According to the *Legal Times*, the Morgan case typifies his reputation as a stern disciplinarian and tough sentencer who is un-sympathetic to women's issues. On the bench he is said to exhibit a very controlled demeanor. He is rigid, dignified, stubborn, not given to outbursts. Foretich's evaluation of Judge Dixon's behavior is noteworthy. He feels that the judge has been extraor-dinarily patient, prudent, contemplative. He had Hil-ary's best interest at heart. Morgan forced his hand. He gave her every chance, but she was utterly defiant and not respectful in any way. She ridiculed and sneered at him, but he did not let himself be pro-voked.

I can well imagine that Judge Dixon lacked the sense of humor to understand and deal with that fireball of a woman, who is the very opposite of rigid-ity. I can also well imagine that it did not need much reconnoitering for her to get a picture of the weak-nesses he covers with a mask of crabbiness. I get the picture of a man who laughs heartily only once a year, if at all. I am almost certain that Morgan let him feel her low esteem unmercifully. To be sure, the Morgan-Foretich dispute cannot have been an easy matter for him. He had been on the bench for only half a year when he first heard Morgan v. Foretich, and he had never dealt with a child molestation case. He is said to have stated publicly more than once that he finds the allegation of child abuse repugnant. Dr. Froning observed what may have been only all too significant: when, as a witness, she demonstrated how Hilary used the anatomically correct dolls to show what her father had done to her, the Judge was unable to toler-ate the sight and turned away. There are reasons other than conflict of interest that ought to make a judge resign from a case.

If I now turn to the Lord's interlocution with King Solomon, I am not so far away from the subject matter, as the reader will soon realize. In any case, it may recommend itself to be perused by Judge Dixon. According to the Bible, the Lord appeared to Solomon, the King of Israel who lived in the 10th century B.C., "in a dream by night; and God said 'Ask what I shall give you.' " Solomon was humble and asked for an understanding mind, so that he might discern good and evil. The Lord was moved by Solomon's humbleness and gave him "a wise and discerning mind" as had never existed before nor will ever exist again (1 Kings 3:5–12). Shortly thereafter two harlots appeared before Solomon's throne; both had given birth to a son, one of whom had died, and each mother claimed the living child for herself.

> Then the king said, "The one says, 'This is my son that is alive, and your son is dead'; and the other says, 'No; but your son is dead, and my son is the living one'." And the king said, "Bring me a sword." So a sword was brought before the king. And the king said, "Divide the living child in two, and give half to the one, and half to the other." Then the woman whose son was alive said to the king, because her heart yearned for her son, "Oh, my lord, give her the living child, and by no means slay it." But the other said, "It shall be neither mine nor yours; divide it." Then the king answered and said, "Give the living child to the first woman, and by no means slay it; she is the mother" [1 Kings 3:23–27].

This story has rightly become famous. An inscrutable, Gordian-knot situation of hopeless, perplexing tragedy found a solution. With one stroke disequilibrium was converted into equilibrium. No trace of doubt was possible about the identity of the mother, which had an instance before appeared shrouded in impenetrable darkness. This was accomplished in the twinkling of an eye by a wise, empathic mind.

Oddly enough, as soon as the king had stated his ruling that the child be divided, he had to revoke it. Paradoxes have long since lost their standing in the practice of judges. Nowadays, of course, an expert, by using modern genetics, would be able to determine with something like 99 percent or so probability who the natural mother was. King Solomon's verdict was superior to the contemporary one because it was based on 100 percent certainty. It had, however, one great disadvantage: it did not bear repetition and thus did not lend itself as a foundation for a general principle applicable to other instances of its kind. Once mothers knew Solomon's test of true motherhood, the false mother, too, would object to the infant's being cut in half, and the king would have faced the same dilemma that Judge Dixon faced.

Biological expertise does not always assure the victory of justice. Charlie Chaplin, if I recall correctly, was declared by a California court to be the father of a child even though blood tests proved he could not possibly have sired it. According to California law at the time, such tests were not admissible in the determination of paternity.

Here a strange impediment in the U.S. judiciary becomes apparent. The maximal effort at truth-finding is often severely curtailed. It is shocking to hear that throughout the whole course of the Morgan-Foretich custody controversy the fact of the two sisters showing identical genital injuries, a leading piece of evidence, was never presented to a jury. What was the juridic reason for Judges Dixon and Williams to feel that they could not make the identical findings in both children an operative argument? According to the two Judges, the girl Hilary was supposed to wait for court procedures that would permit the presentation of the full available evidence—which might have taken years—before the final decision on appropriate living conditions for her would be handed down. Courts evidently do not always abide by the principle of finding the truth by the quickest and most reliable way; instead, the process of finding truth is subjected to rules of procedure, formalities and abstractions that are separated by an unbridgeable hiatus from social reality and the live needs of suffering human beings. The wisdom that spoke out of King Solomon's mouth would have been wasted if spoken in Fairfax County or the D.C. Superior Court; it would have been brushed aside and overruled by a pale, meaningless abstraction.

The litigation, however, is typical: the father asserting innocence, the mother convinced of past sexual abuse, the experts divided. The judge indeed faces Solomon's dilemma. A strictly codified legal system seems to work against wisdom and empathy. Solomon would have looked sharply at parents fighting over their daughter's body. He probably would have considered the father's several failed marriages, which he might have taken as a sign of instability.

What would have surprised Solomon profoundly is Dr. Foretich's stated conviction that Dr. Morgan is insane. This charge, if true, would recoil on Foretich himself. One is forced to ask: what kind of person would acquiesce in a prolonged imprisonment of his daughter's mother, knowing that she suffers from a serious disorder? He must have known that every additional day in jail might gravely endanger the future of a patient suffering from a disease of that gravity. Was he not tormented by the prospect that Hilary, as an adult, would have to deal with a mother whose mind, gravely disordered as he alleges, had been ravaged by years in prison?

Foretich might have advanced in his favor, against Solomon's way of reasoning, his readiness to give a reward of $50,000 to anyone who could tell him of Hilary's whereabouts. As noted before, according to him, if anyone it was he, not Morgan, who was victimized: events have ruined his name, taken all his income and severely damaged his practice. Solomon, however, might not be too impressed, because most of these sufferings were not caused by sacrifices the father was ready to make but were forced upon him by circumstances. Foretich insists that he would not have fought so hard to contact his little girl if he had been guilty; his lawyers agree with him and see as the most compelling evidence of his innocence his concern for Hilary and his attempts to locate her. One of them is said to have made this astounding statement: "If he had really done all those terrible things, he would be perfectly happy with the situation as it is—Hilary gone, Dr. Morgan in jail. Why is he fighting so hard if he isn't innocent?"

Did Judge Dixon feel inclined to find such absurd reasoning plausible? King Solomon, I am sure, would not have done so. If that is really the most compelling evidence of innocence, the doctor's defense rests on shaky ground. One can hardly evade the suspicion that Foretich is a self-righteous man. If I grasp the legal situation correctly, all he would have had to do was to agree to supervised visitation, and the child's mother would have been spared prison, while he would have known Hilary's whereabouts and would have been able to meet her at regular intervals. Another point might have interested Solomon: in view of the father's anguish over being separated from his younger daughter, Solomon might have been surprised to notice that he tolerated not having seen his older daughter for several years. Foretich, when confronted with that discrepancy, responded that he knew Jane was doing all right, whereas this was not assured about Hilary. Was there really a reason to fear that the grandparents would neglect their granddaughter?

Solomon, always interested in motives, and measuring their sincerity in terms of the hardship a person was ready to suffer, would be deeply moved by the length to which the mother was going in bearing hardship in order to protect her offspring. In contrast, Foretich's lawyers depict Morgan's stay in prison as a kind of El Dorado: a mother who does not have to take care of her child; a doctor who does not have to take care of patients; and a fiancée (Morgan was engaged at the time of imprisonment) who does not have to participate in candlelight dinners. According to this appalling cynicism, lawyers would have to do their best to get their clients into jail, where they could evade the plights attached to an existence in freedom.

Solomon would perhaps ask: Why was the litigating party unready to agree to supervised visitation?—the inconvenience that it caused would not measure up to a fraction of what the mother was willing to endure. Does the father perhaps respond

with such self-righteousness and insistence on unsupervised visitation because he is unwilling to bear
the stigma of suspicion? By accepting supervision he
certainly would not have admitted guilt. True, an innocent man might understandably object to supervised visitation; still, rather than risk separation from
his child and imprisonment of his former wife, both
for an extensive period of time, one would expect him
to accept the restraint. The suspicion of abuse persists
in any case, whether he accepts or fights supervised
visitation. When he indignantly retorts: "I am not
letting some woman in jail run my life," he oddly
enough made it possible that some woman in jail *was*
running his life.

In weighing against each other the sacrifices father
and mother were ready to make, Solomon would decide in favor of the child's mother. In our times, in
which litigants cannot count on being met by Solomon's wisdom, recourse is taken to the expert who
is expected to furnish incontrovertible proof of fact.
The expert's testimony in modern times is surrounded by the halo that was attached to the ancient
ordeals of trials by fire, water, and combat, and all
the other superstitious paraphernalia to which con-
testants in bygone times had to bow. The list of expert
witnesses on which Morgan based her request of supervised visitation is formidable and, once heard, not
likely to be forgotten, but experts do not always
agree. As noted before, this happened also in the
Morgan-Foretich custody case.

Therefore, one might have expected Judge Dixon
to pay obeisance to a generally accepted peculiarity
of our judicial system. Another judge might have
reached a more suitable verdict, for in a tribunal the

decision as to whether an action is right or wrong depends in most important issues not on the merit of the case but on a majority vote. Although it is not supported by reason that the verdict of two justices is implicitly superior to the one who disagrees with the majority, this bias in favor of numbers is deeply rooted in the thinking of Western society. One might have thought, therefore, that Judge Dixon would have preferred the testimony of the eleven or so experts who were certain of abuse over the opinions of the four who denied it.

Judge Dixon may have rejected the majority and felt unable to end the state of equipoise because of the uncertainty that always hangs over events that happen behind closed doors, an uncertainty that is particularly pronounced when love and affection are at play. Certainty about the degree of intimacy to which amorous affairs have advanced is rare. To give but one classical example: Upon his arrival in Weimar, Goethe fell in love with Frau von Stein, seven years his senior, married, and mother of six children, three of whom had survived. For a decade she acted as the dominant figure in his life. Their relationship was no secret: the Court and the couple's friends knew of it and it was discussed by contemporaries, with contradictory inferences. The secondary literature is equally filled with explorations of their liaison, and yet scholars still have not reached agreement on the nature of their closeness, though Goethe's passionate letters have been preserved. And I doubt that inferences would be essentially better secured if the inamorata's letters, too, had reached posterity.

In cases of abuse in which children are involved, the effort to establish the truth is even more difficult than in instances of adult love. First of all, there is the question of the reliability of children's testimony. On occasion, it is true, children are surprisingly effective as witnesses—they respond to details that may escape an adult. But they are devastatingly suggestible. One can never be certain that they do not take their own fantasy as the memory of an event that took place in outer reality. This confounding of inner and outer reality occurs even in adults—and not so rarely, for that matter—and children are far less endowed to distinguish between these two realities, particularly under the stressful conditions of parental discord. Thus it must be asked whether one should trust the testimony of the older sister, Jane, when she describes an abuse by her father and says that she saw him do the same to her sister. Although the American Bar Association found that deliberately false allegations by adults are rare in cases of child abuse, one cannot be quite certain that when a child describes graphically what a father did to her or forced her to do, an irate or vindictive mother has not coached her to report incriminating events. A mother may inadvertently instill in a child's mind the seed of what later becomes a realistic report of exposure to abuse; a child may even respond to a mother's unconscious fantasies, wishes and desires to compromise the father. A mother may precipitate a choice of images in a child by a simple question, depending on the emotions operating within her while asking. The child's unconscious is often excessively smart in absorbing feelings of which the adult is unaware and which would be denied indignantly and yet do exist. To avoid misunderstanding—nothing of that sort has been reported and nothing suggests its operation in

Hilary, which, however, would not disprove the possibility.

At any rate, considerations of the unreliability of children's testimony may have prevented Judge Dixon from accepting as evidence Hilary's play in which dolls carried out all kinds of forbidden things, and all the revelations the child imparted to her mother, the therapist and the testing psychologist. When the Judge declared, despite the mass of evidence accumulated, "The Court is unwilling to find as more probable than not that the alleged abuse occurred or did not occur," he raised a question but did not answer it: Which kind of evidence in a child abuse case would, or should, induce a judge to find it more probable than not that the alleged abuse had occurred and thus end the state of equipoise?

The concept of admissibility of evidence has its proper, well-defined place in jury trials. What is not admissible never comes, or should never come, to a jury's attention. However, when Judge Dixon faced the situation of having to make up his mind on supervised versus unsupervised visitations, he was under no obligation to put on record the full compass of evidence he considered in arriving at his decision. Something that may have been inadmissible in a trial by jury might nevertheless have directed his thinking. Nothing could have prevented him from taking Jane's genital injury into consideration. The remarkable feature of his decision in favor of unsupervised visitation is that he knew of the half-sister's identical injury. Could he really prevent his mind from taking cognizance of the existence of aggravating circumstances? Does the doctrine of inadmissibility include the demand that a judge must not extend awareness to existing reality? After all, in that fateful ruling to let the father be with the child for two weeks without supervision, he was not obliged to defend his decision; and he would not have had to, if he had decided in favor of supervision. The parties had to accept his decision *tel quel*. Does a judge's thinking have to be so rigidly compartmentalized in legalistic categories that he is totally uninfluenced by the existence of a smoking gun that, even though inadmissible in a jury trial, is right before his eyes?

At any rate, it is useful to speculate what evidence Judge Dixon might have accepted as conclusive. I feel impelled to infer that only one or all of the following would have lived up to his presumptive standard of conclusiveness: a defendant's confession; the testimony of a competent, trustworthy adult witness; identification of the abuser's sperm found in or upon the child's body or clothes. If conclusive evidence of child abuse should be limited to such narrow factors, it would provide relief to perpetrators since none of the three factors is likely to occur. The chances of ever establishing conclusive evidence of paternal abuse—or abuse by anybody, for that matter—would be greatly reduced. Fathers who feel inclined toward sexual abuse of their infant daughters might feel encouraged and reasonably assured that their misdeeds will never be followed by embarrassing consequences; they will rarely be prosecuted, let alone sentenced.

Does this mean that a judge who faces a situation of equipoise, as Judge Dixon was sure he did, had no means at his disposal for reaching a decision other than to toss a coin and perpetrate arbitrariness? Such circumstances do not necessarily create a chaotic situation in which the fate of a little girl is left unchecked to accidental vagaries. After all, conclusive evidence would make a father a criminal. In custody cases mothers do not aim at their ex-spouses' imprisonment. What they want is only a decision on whether father and daughter ought to spend some time together without supervision. It stands to reason that for a decree of supervised visitation the mere suspicion of abuse should suffice, or else a decree of supervised visitation would be tantamount to a finding of a criminal offense, which such a decree definitely is not. By substituting *suspicion* for *conclusive evidence* as the focal issue in cases of custody litigation of the Morgan-Foretich kind, the problem becomes manageable.

One of Judge Dixon's shortcomings was his failure to anticipate the predictable state of desperate anguish that his ruling would necessarily produce in the mother. A mother cannot be expected to leave her daughter alone with a father who is suspected of sexual abuse. How then did he anticipate a mother to act who was told by 11 experts—rightly or wrongly is not at issue here—that her daughter had been molested repeatedly, who was even told by one of them that one more unsupervised visit with the father would be risking suicide? Could such a mother go home and tell her daughter, "Pack your satchel, darling, join your daddy for two weeks, and when you come back, tell your mummy what happened"? In addition, Judge Dixon knew from objective witnesses such as Savage and Holman about the child's frenzied reactions to the prospect of being alone with her father. Was Morgan supposed to tell her daughter,

"Nice girls do whatever a father tells them to do. Uncle Judge will tell you later that you only imagined those bad things or that only 50 percent of them took place"? After all, Judge Dixon knew of the protection Hilary's half-sister received from his colleague in nearby Fairfax County. What gave him the certainty of being so much more discriminating? Did he really expect that the mother would remain inactive and wait until conclusive evidence had been obtained, which might have taken months or even years, if indeed, as pointed out above, conclusive evidence as Judge Dixon apparently defined it would have been obtainable at all? Should Morgan have overruled 11 experts and relied on the doubts of a judge who is not trained as an expert in the precarious field of child abuse? In the light of these questions it sounds like bitter irony, or like the intention to hurt the mother as deeply as possible, when Judge Dixon pronounced: "As each day passes, Dr. Morgan misses an opportunity to be part of her child's life. The learning experiences in school, the celebration of a birthday or Christmas or Mother's Day, or the opportunity to comfort the child after a scrape or fall. As each day passes, Dr. Morgan is confronted with the fact that she can walk out of jail any time she wants." Without bias one may state that Judge Dixon has not the faintest notion of human sentiments.

In substituting *suspicion* for *conclusive evidence*, the nature of the problem seems to have changed face. However, there is a substantial drawback involved. Suspicion is a vague notion that is all too readily provoked; it is not so infrequent that suspicion can be traced to the suspecting person's conflicts, wishes and imagery rather than to the suspected person's behavior. Whereas conclusive evidence is certainly too narrow a demand, the concept of suspicion seems too broad. It needs a qualifier, such as "justified," or it may be categorized as "reasonable doubt." If the Morgan case were typical, there should be no difficulty, for the consensus of 11 experts creates, if not certainty, at least a state of justified suspicion or reasonable doubt—unless one assumes conspiracy, of which no one seriously thought besides Foretich. However, the consensus of 11 experts is a rare conjuncture that cannot generally be expected. Evidently, situations of uncertainty about the existence of justified suspicion will occur. But such uncertainty, as noted, was not present in the last phase of the Morgan-Foretich litigation, after Judge Dixon had ruled that a state of equipoise existed. Equipoise of evidence that does not entail justified suspicion of the male in question is a contradiction in itself. Admittedly, conclusive evidence is superior to justified suspicion as far as preciseness is concerned: one of three well-defined particulars I have specified above has to be present. But the superiority of preciseness fades in the light of its narrow applicability. One cannot count on clear-cut definitions in reaching a decision as to what is necessary for a child's welfare. Because it reduces the risk of damage to the child, preference must be given to justified suspicion in decisions regarding a father's right of unsupervised visitation.

The child's welfare remained oddly undiscussed in the proceedings before Judge Dixon; it ought, of course, to have been the central issue. As soon as Judge Dixon advanced the idea that a state of equipoise existed, he acknowledged his own quandary about what might have happened between father and daughter. A simple line of reasoning will make clear that his personal incertitude made supervised visitation mandatory: if abuse had occurred, one more act would gravely aggravate the psychopathology of the endangered child; if no abuse had ever come to pass, supervised visitation, it is true, would be superfluous, but if carried out in a tactful way it would amount to no more than a negligible inconvenience, without damage to either child or father. If doubt is present, that decision becomes mandatory.

Hilary's welfare was endangered from the beginning by the tension prevalent in her parents' relationship. To this were added the incessant litigation and the frequent genital examinations, tests and explorations centering around the issue of paternal abuse and how far it had gone. All this laid the groundwork for serious psychopathology in the present, and more to be expected later. To be sure, some conditions that mental hygiene would unfailingly call malignant may, surprisingly, bear unanticipated healthy fruit. Isaac Newton serves as an example that even grave infantile traumata do not stand in the way of, perhaps even favor, the development of a child's mind into an adult who would leave forever a mark on civilization. One of my patients showed a high degree of creativity and facility to adjust, yet she had an alcoholic mother who was promiscuous and brought home inebriated lovers.

Still, one cannot rely on the exceptional in decisions of the day and has to place one's trust in the average. Strange as it may seem, I would suggest, tentatively, that Judge Dixon may have inadvertently done Hilary a service. Disregarding the terrible price her mother had to pay, her removal to the care of grandparents—let us hope they are affectionate and reasonable—might have been a turn that was optimal for her. In view of the conditions at home, which were potentially damaging, there is no reason to doubt that the grandparents have provided her with a more stable, peaceful and favorable environment than her mother would have been able to offer, even if Judge Dixon had decided favorably on supervised visitations. The ruling Morgan requested would not have protected the little girl from further traumatization, which is unavoidable when parents are invariably at cross-purposes. Children are victims of the virulent acerbity that parents feel toward each other, even when they are living separated. Hilary's parents were irreconcilably kept apart by extreme ill-feelings. Under these circumstances the older Morgans, even though they themselves had gone through a hostile divorce, would have a good chance of providing a more promising setting for Hilary than could have been established in Washington, whatever the Court decided.

The separation from the natural mother may be compensated by grandmotherly affection; on the other hand, one must fear that the necessary secrecy of identity, which I assume was forced upon Hilary by an undercover existence, could lay the foundation of a later ego-disturbance. But even here one makes surprising observations. I was told of a Jewish child who was brought up during World War II in an occupied country and had to conceal name and identity for years in order to escape racial persecution. Later she showed no signs of unusual pathology of identity. However, the child spent all that underground time in close proximity to her mother.

The climate of the time may sway opinion. It has been maintained that mothers are frequently denied credence because men harbor a collective unwillingness to believe that a father could involve himself in the guilt of sexually abusing his own child. One has attributed to Judge Dixon such unwillingness, which seems to be present in most males. However, we may stand at a watershed and approach a time when the majority will not hesitate to uncritically believe incriminations against fathers, which nowadays are raised with increasing frequency.

Dr. Morgan, for her part—whatever her unconscious conflicts and ambivalences may be—can maintain persuasively that she acted in Hilary's best interest. Convinced of paternal abuse, she thought it to be her duty to protect the infant under all circumstances. Any other procedure would have made her a coward—in her eyes, and possibly in reality—and would have exposed her to the later accusation by her adult daughter of having overruled the opinion of 11 experts and destroyed forever her child's happiness by giving in to what the daughter would then call the blind verdict of an unknowledgeable, blind judge.

However, there was a voice that potently superseded any positive statement that could be made about Morgan and her motives. It came from one of the experts called in by Dr. Foretich: Dr. Elissa Benedek, professor of psychiatry and, at the time of her testimony, president elect of the American Psychiatric Association. But first a few remarks about the present standing of psychiatric expert testimony in court.

Distrust in the reliability of psychiatrists when they function as forensic experts is the rule. The scene of one testifying for the prosecution—asserting responsibility of the defendant—and the other, for the defense—diagnosing a disturbance that would free the defendant of accountability—is a spectacle that is as disconcerting as it is frequent. It lies in the nature of things, which Dostoevsky succinctly exposed when he said that psychology is a stick with two ends. What is accessible to direct sense-perception and measurable cannot be doubted. Psychic elements are not as perceptible as those of the physical order; the presence and impact of emotions are always open to doubt. Therefore it happened that, while other scientific discoveries have been most profitably applied in forensic medicine, and many fields have delivered tools indispensable at present for the proof of a defendant's guilt or innocence, psychiatry has not been equally successful in securing a respectable place in that procedure. Its findings have not been accepted in the courtroom with the same readiness as those of other sciences. Dissension exists in every science, but it is usually of a passing nature, whereas the opposing views of psychiatrists in forensic matters are a constant feature in the courtroom and will persist for the indefinite future.

A bizarre situation from my own experience will illustrate this complexity and ambiguity. As a neuropsychiatrist in the United States Army during World War II, one of my duties was to assess the mental status and responsibility of defendants, usually young trainees who had gone AWOL. This required the submission of a written opinion and a hearing before a Board. In the former I felt obliged to follow the timeworn, printed Army regulations regarding accountability, but when under oath before the

Board, I was convinced I had the moral obligation to state my personal conviction, which almost always was the opposite of what the Army regulations on my desk wanted to have enforced. There was no doubt in my mind that those wretched youngsters, who within the shortest time had been thrown from their peaceful, genial surroundings into a psychologically barbaric, unempathetic world, and who felt that an early death was waiting for them, were unable to "adhere to the right," as well as to resist the impulse to quit camp, which ended in their being prosecuted. I am certain King Solomon, with a twinkle in his eye, would have forgiven my duplicity, which to my good fortune never came to the authorities' attention.

But let me now turn to Dr. Benedek's testimony. She had been vocal in the past about her conviction that most sexual-abuse accusations in child cases were unfounded. She stated in court that she did not find any convincing psychological evidence that Hilary had been sexually molested. The reliability of her testimony was doubted. She has relatively little psychiatric experience with children. When she examined Hilary she used the conjoint interview—that is, she spoke with the child, not alone but in her father's presence. This is a controversial technique because an abused child will more frequently than not try to please the father she is confronting. A child younger than five years old can hardly be expected to admit to abuse in the presence of the perpetrator, especially if he is endowed with paternal authority. Furthermore, Benedek was asked in court whether the abuse of a sibling by a parent would make that of a second sibling more likely. She denied knowledge of studies proving that it did, even though, as I am told, there are several such investigations indicating an 80 percent likelihood. Perhaps even more perplexing is the following statement she is supposed to have made:

> I am convinced that most people who allege abuse really believe that it happened and want to protect their child. But there are some cases where a professional says "this is highly unlikely," and people find another professional to validate the abuse. You shop around long enough, you may be able to find one.

When she limited the opprobrious "shopping around" to "some cases," did she have in mind that it occurs only in rare cases? If so, why did she bring up the exceptional before a jury? At any rate, her remark sheds a doubtful light on psychiatric expertise in general. If she were right, it would bring discredit upon any psychiatric testimony. By using the disparaging term of "shopping around" she implies that psychiatrists can be actuated to testify in favor of their clients, whatever the clinical situation may be.

If Dr. Benedek's belief in the unreliability of psychiatric testimony swayed a court against Hilary's mother, she should be asked for the evidence she possessed that Dr. Morgan had shopped around. Note that she did not say that mothers turn in despair from one psychiatrist toward another until they find one who takes pity on them; instead, she uses a pejorative vernacular, and by doing so she suggests the venality of psychiatric witnesses in general. Her remark was evidently meant as a reference to Morgan, in which case it is oddly out of place. As noted earlier, as soon as the mother's suspicion crystallized, she turned to a child psychiatrist; and it was he who, though not confirming abuse, referred the mother to a social worker, whose examination of the two sisters determined abuse. Judge Dixon consented to Hilary's examination at the Chesapeake Institute. One really cannot call that "shopping around," and Dr. Benedek should have specified the procedures parents ought to follow in order to live up to her standards. The possibly oblique nature of psychiatric testimony notwithstanding, Benedek had no right to slight the profession publicly. I consider it an affront when this is done by a person who was elected to be its highest representative. Did Dr. Foretich, by virtue of eleven witnesses against him, and four in his favor, have to do a bit of shopping around of his own, until he found in Dr. Benedek a witness willing to serve in his favor? At any rate, if she were right, no psychiatrist averse to unprofessional behavior could permit himself to function as an expert witness. Her allegations, if verified, would necessitate the immediate drafting of guidelines for judges and psychiatrists.

Every litigant would have to disclose the names of all psychiatric experts he had consulted, as well as the opinion of each. It would further be necessary to determine the reasons for the litigant's choice of a particular expert. Likewise, experts serving as witnesses would have to testify to the nature of their previous relationship with the litigant, as well as to what emoluments they received or expect to receive. After all, why should only prospective jurors be cross-examined regarding their suitability to serve on specific cases? An equivalent cross-examination would be in place when the president of a professional organization has doubts about the integrity of the members that elected her.

With some embarrassment I shall report on that part of Dr. Benedek's testimony that is particularly disconcerting. She told the court that Morgan had been diagnosed by her own psychiatrist, Dr. Carol Kleinman, as having "a mixed personality disorder," which is a disorder of a chronic nature, incurable in general, and showing impairment of some gravity. It was asserted in a few articles that Dr. Kleinman had not made that diagnosis. Suspecting misinformation, I asked Dr. Kleinman for clarification, and I gratefully repeat her answer:

> I did not tell Dr. Benedek that Elizabeth Morgan suffered from "a mixed personality disorder." I spoke with Dr. Benedek [in December, 1986]. At that time my diagnosis of Dr. Morgan was "Adjustment Disorder with Depressed Mood." She continued in psychotherapy twice a week and my notes indicate that by March 31, 1987, my diagnosis had changed to "No Mental Disorder." When I made my public statements I was referring to the mental condition after the Adjustment Disorder had resolved. I never found her to be "disturbed." I felt that she responded appropriately considering the stress that she was under. My recollection is that I communicated that to Dr. Benedek [private communication of February 6, 1990].

I do hope Dr. Benedek was not under oath when she made the statement about Morgan's alleged personality disorder. Whether this was technically perjury or not, it is most distressing to find out that the president of the American Psychiatric Association made herself guilty of a severe misrepresentation. She became partisan when it was her duty to preserve the strictest objectivity. She damaged Morgan seriously by casting doubt on her reliability as a witness and as a responsible mother. Her distortion of facts is particularly revolting since it was done to the detriment of a woman smarting under a catastrophic upheaval of her existence.

The public's response to Morgan's incarceration gives cause for some comments. According to one survey, most males considered Morgan mentally disturbed, and Foretich innocent and disadvantaged. This response supposedly is determined by the disbelief of upper-middle-class males that other middle-class males would molest their own children. The explanation is probably valid, but it would be dimsighted to let the matter rest there. After all, a judge was holding a woman in prison without trial and declared, after a year and a half, that coercion had only just begun; the possibility threatened that this coercion might be extended to last for a decade, if not longer, until the woman's daughter would come of age. Did this procedure not smack of the good old Star Chamber proceedings? Understandably this gave rise to alarm abroad, and the Inter-American Commission on Human Rights sent a telegram to the Secretary of State questioning "whether a citizen can be kept indefinitely in jail, accused of no crime, from a secret trial all records sealed." Should one not have expected an explosion of wrath, with millions of letters pouring into the White House, Capitol Hill, the Court, to the Judge, particularly when the victim is a woman, a mother? Should one not have expected that, in men, the sense of chivalry was challenged and, in women, the sense of offended motherhood? After all, here was a woman who was not asking for a favor but merely a ruling stating that a witness be present when the father meets with her daughter, a father who had been prohibited by a neighboring court from meeting his other daughter at all unless he obtained permission from the daughter's therapist. It may have looked as though waves of protest finally led to Morgan's discharge, but in reality her incarceration aroused only ripples. After all, millions of citizens read about her atrocious plight and they did not become infuriated by that revolting miscarriage of justice. It took a rather long time before a protest got off the ground. One may speak of a relative lethargy that is alarming and ominous.

The Morgan case seems to me to be the symptom of a deeper process that should arouse and alert the body politic. When a judge has the power and right to keep an innocent woman detained in jail for years, something is profoundly wrong in our judicial system, and the present safeguards against judicial excesses evidently do not suffice. This judge demanded total surrender to a dictum that was arbitrary, since it was in open contradiction to, and overruled, the explicit statement of a substantial number of accredited experts regarding an imperative measure for the maintenance of a child's minimal health standards. By his action the judge not only endangered a child's mental health: he also trampled on a woman's natural rights. The refusal to respect a mother's minimal right is most alarming. Does it foreshadow a similar assault against the rights of women in general? Since this is a problem with far-reaching implications, it demands close attention. A discussion must be inserted here regarding women's rights and related issues.

EXCURSUS ON THE SUPREME COURT, ABORTION AND THE DEATH PENALTY

Shifting one's gaze from the tight local fabric of the Morgan-Foretich custody litigation to the national scene, one feels impelled to ask: Are the 759 days of Morgan's incarceration the result of a fortuitous encounter between a rigid judge and a provocative woman? Or did they bring to the surface a trend in this country that is gradually gaining momentum?

I

Alarmingly, a survey reports that the majority of men questioned were critical of the mother's contempt of court and sided with the Judge. This suggests the ominous conclusion that the Judge's anti-female attitude echoed widely in the male population. Women no longer disposed to accept their wretched, age-old lot face an up-hill struggle.

The foundation of men's overbearing insolence toward women can be traced to their greater physical strength, which enables them to force women into sexual submission. Civilization would be expected to undo the effects of this crude biological factor, and has, in fact, partially done so. But although sexual arbitrariness has been restrained, discrimination, exploitation, and other wrongful acts continue to be observed throughout the world.

Women's protest, their organized resistance to male domination, have varied in the course of history. In the last few decades, revolutionary changes that legislation should have effected long ago were sanctioned under the relentless pressure of the Women's Liberation Movement and like organizations. In 1973, when the Supreme Court ruled that abortion is a constitutional right, a momentous victory was won. In view of the macabre procession of victims of ineptly performed abortions, as well as of women forced to endure anguish and humiliation by unwanted pregnancies, in consequence often being driven to take their own lives, this ruling was an apogee of agape, a victory of Christian humanity. At long last a woman was given liberty to make her own decisions regarding the most decisive issue in her life.

Nevertheless, deliberate interruption of pregnancy for nonmedical reasons is nowadays considered a crime by many. Contemporary forces that so categorize abortion are strong, and it seems questionable whether the right of free choice will survive. When social processes have advanced toward relative freedom, the danger of a backlash arises. Germany's Weimar Republic contributed significantly to the emancipation of women, but this move forward was rudely undone by the National Socialist government, which initiated a regression leading to its extreme opposite. Surprisingly, the National Socialist Party, despite its pledge to enact reactionary laws against women, received ample support from the female vote in the elections that led to the *Machtübernahme*—Hitler's seizure of power. It is questionable whether Hitler would have become Chancellor if the majority of women had stuck to the parties that opposed him. Do we in this country have to fear the rise to dominance of a movement determined to undo the hard-won victories of emancipation and civil rights, which are inseparably bound together?

Was Judge Dixon's eager and unflinching determination to incarcerate Morgan for years—longer than thieves or drug dealers have been held for their misdeeds—was that determination, so truculently directed at a woman innocent of an offense, based exclusively on judiciary considerations? Or was it an indication that the backlash that had been simmering since 1973 was intensifying? One would be eager to know whether what impressed so many as the Judge's vindictiveness was aroused by Morgan's behavior, or whether he was dazzled and felt betrayed in his male pride when he was confronted with the radiance of her superstardom. Her position in the national limelight as a columnist and author of best-sellers, her practicing in a profession previously reserved for men, and her income, which probably exceeded his own—all that had been made possible by the emancipation that has deeply stirred women's lives. One also has to weigh idiosyncrasies frequently encountered in males when a woman's professionalism and independence do not keep her from enjoying motherhood. The prerogatives nature gave women in procreating and raising children are causes of men's mostly unconscious, unending envy of them. Morgan, at the time her case came before Judge Dixon, could well serve as a symbol of all the blessings emancipation has brought to American womanhood after suffragettes had assured the female vote. When Judge Dixon saw Morgan last, however, she had been brought to her knees: glamour had vanished, she was unemployed, deprived of funds, unproductive, disheveled, separated from her child, and in the company of prostitutes and addicts. Despite these calamities she was staunch and in strong spirits, far from whining—and the Judge's reaction was his solemn assurance that her incarceration to that point was only a beginning.

Even if I read too much into a simple contempt-of-court order and the Judge was merely defending the legal right of courts to adjudicate a case, it is proper to sound an alarm: his actions and the relative public apathy foreshadow dangers for a movement that aspires to equality in all walks of life and the constitutional assurance of free choice.

II

This brings us back to the right to interruption of pregnancy, on which emancipation centers. As long as the right of free choice is secure, the foundation of female freedom is warranted. No other right, with the exception of suffrage, is as important in providing women with a feeling of unthreatened identity, of being free and therefore the masters of their own

future. However, that the right to interruption is protected by the Constitution is in dispute, and even the
prohibition of interventions that were permitted prior
to 1973 is being demanded. A large group of gynecol-
ogists refuses to perform abortions, and some even
object to prenatal exploration of the fetus to detect
defective genes. As one said: "Some families are
made a lot stronger by letting a Down's child be born"
(*The New York Times*, September 8, 1991). The psychological and physical risks of abortion are stressed although it is assured that both are low. One does not
discover convincing arguments raised by opponents
of intervention. The unconscious background of opposition to abortion has not yet been sufficiently clarified. It is possible that the nucleus of that opposition
is a derivative of an early aggressive impulse against
a pregnant mother or her substitute, resulting in a
deep-seated and frightening feeling of shame and
guilt, but I doubt the general validity of that hypothesis.

I shall have more to say about the right-to-life
movement but turn now to the arguments that have
been raised against free choice. Perhaps the principal
one is the equation of abortion with murder. Finnis
(1973, p. 144) maintains "that the unborn child is
[from conception on] a person." If this could be
proved, or made plausible, it would be clear that interruption is murder. When Thompson (1971, p. 47)
calls it a "slippery argument," she is mild in her criticism. It is impossible to attribute to a cell the singular-
ity of a person. Uniqueness of structure does not suffice to define a person. No two amoebas are identical
in structure. Not only does each organism have its
own structure, which makes it different from others

of its species in some detail, insignificant as it may be: even a crystal is individually distinguishable. One may venture to speculate that, if the measurements were feasible, atoms of the same element and even electrons would display some differences. Saint Thomas Aquinas held that in the early phases of gestation the embryo has no soul. The idea of a soulless and brainless cell being a person is a contrariety in itself, indeed an absurdity. Interruption of pregnancy amounts in all instances to destruction of a potential human person; however, to equate a potentiality with the end product, as Finnis does, will not be generally accepted. If destruction of an embryo is murder, ought one not to classify the avoidance of forming potential human life in much the same way?[4]

The murder-abortion thesis was never accepted in this country. Even when abortion was prohibited, offenders were not charged with murder. Requests to permit abortion in cases of rape, incest and constitutional defect are common. In making such requests, it is acknowledged that abortion is not murder, which is disallowed under all circumstances.

The murder theory, being dubious, cannot be acknowledged as binding on the community at large. The same is true of religious and ethical arguments, which are acknowledged as valid principles of behavior by individual groups but do not touch upon unnegotiable fundamental principles. The content of most pamphlets objecting to free choice is limited to the large number of "murders" of children alleged to occur in this country and to frightening photos of fetuses in the womb.

[4]As a matter of fact, many theologians equated contraception with murder and judged it to be a sin worse than incest (cf. Ranke-Heinemann, 1990, pp. 177–215).

I turn now to a few of the arguments in favor of freedom of choice. Demographers leave little doubt that overpopulation is a danger to mankind's survival. When the Lord promised Abraham that his descendants would be as numerous as the dust of the earth and the stars (Genesis 13:16 and 15:5), He overreached Himself. The world He created is too small for such a project,[5] as it is when vast populations are deprived of family planning, which includes abortion. The prohibition of interruption in most thirdworld countries enforces resort to inept techniques, leading to 200 fatalities a day. Fatalities of the same sort were not rare in this country before the ruling of 1973.

In early phases of mankind's history human beings were the most precious commodity. Their small number left it open to doubt whether the human species would survive. Sparingly developed technology was no match for the perfectly developed instincts of hostile animals endowed with superior strength, nor a protection against the many treacherous ways of existence. Today the reverse is true. Technology and its foolish application threaten the survival of many species, and it is overpopulation that calls man's survival into question; technology is on the verge of devouring nature and, consequently, also man. The Great Flood

---

[5]God's injunction to "be fruitful and multiply" (Genesis 1:28) had an enormous effect. According to Augustine, intercourse without intent and possibility of pregnancy is a mortal sin. It seems to me that mankind contributed its fair share in carrying out that injunction. There is no indication that the Lord had in mind that there should be no upper limit to multiplication. In truth, mankind multiplied enormously as soon as science reduced the infant mortality that prevailed during centuries of greatest religious fervor. It might impress believers as a paradox that science, which is the main cause of the decline of religion, nevertheless contributed so much to the survival of infants.

once protected nature against man, but this time the Lord leaves nature undefended.

There are many actions which, although they are illegal, cannot be prevented; interruption of pregnancy, were it to be prohibited, would be one of them. Just as prohibition did not stamp out alcohol consumption, so was interruption never stamped out while it was against the law. This has erroneously been used as an argument in favor of free choice. Murder, strangely enough, is a crime that cannot be extirpated either. It is difficult to understand why this has to be, but it is safe to predict that as long as people live together in groups, incidents of fatal violence will occur. Yet it would assuredly be an error to conclude that therefore murder should go unpunished. And yet a prohibition of interruption would be a grave injustice for the simple reason that the wealthy, any prohibitions notwithstanding, would go on enjoying the privilege of safe abortion on demand. It would be like permitting the wealthy to commit murder whenever the impulse seizes them. Kate Simon reports (1982, p. 70) that her mother, living under difficult economic conditions, went through 13 abortions that were performed by a competent physician at a time when interruption was prosecuted. This is exceptional and there is no doubt that making abortion illegal would bar only the economically weak from safe abortion.

Whatever reasons in favor of freedom of choice exist, they do not contribute to a compromise between opponents. The pragmatic point of view does not end the controversy when law, ethics and religion are given the last word. The Catholic dogma prohibits interruption under all conditions, even at the price of the mother's life. Yet it is usually overlooked that a religious sentiment may, even though only rarely, be the very driving force toward interruption. I shall outline two types of situations in which this might happen.

Times have changed and sinning, starting at an early age, is rampant throughout the Western world. On good grounds, a pregnant woman might be convinced that the chances of her progeny's dying in grace are negligible. For a good enough mother, the prospect of her child's suffering in purgatory or eternal hell is bound to arouse horror, and interruption will become mandatory. She will be unselfish enough to commit a mortal sin for the sake of rescuing the one whom she would love most. Her own torment in hell, which she expects, will be borne by her with the fortitude that behooves a Christian saint. Dogma apart, such a woman would have the disposition of a truly good mother, and one would have to admire her for denying herself both the incomparable joys of maternal intimacy with a newborn as well as the prospect of ever entering Heaven. Only too late might she find out that, according to dogma, her sacrifice was in vain. Original sin is inherited, and the soul is contaminated from the moment of conception. Thus, whether it be a case of miscarriage or abortion, the fetus is destined for eternal perdition, unless use is made of the baptismal syringe that was invented by theologians for cleansing the fetus of original sin when in danger of expiring in utero. In the interval between baptism and an immediately following abortion, the soul would indeed be protected against the commission of sin. Such an arrangement would provide the mother with absolute certainty of her child's triumphant appearance in Heaven.

In the second situation, which is historical, abortion serving a holy intent was practiced by dissidents who were deeply anguished by the fact that man's sinful conduct exposes God to pain. They knew that humanity is ineluctably fated to aggrieve the Lord, and in order to spare Him grief, propagation had to be terminated. The cessation of propagation is indeed the only way in which sinning will ever come to an end, necessitating the availability of abortion. No convincing argument against that sect's reasoning has yet been discovered.

These two illustrations make it evident that interruption of pregnancy may serve purposes that are exclusively and unquestionably religious and ethical, and is not necessarily selfish, as so many claim. Therefore, prohibition of interruption may contravene ethical behavior. Religious reasoning, too, has not led to a generally acceptable resolution of the problem. Posner wisely remarked,

> With the decline of authority and the rise of independent thinking a society also becomes morally heterogeneous to the point when people within the same political community may come to inhabit incommensurable moral universes. That is the situation in this country today with respect to the abortion controversy and the reason the controversy seems to admit of no rationally demonstrable resolution [Posner, 1990, p. 129].

Unfortunately, those who feel ready to submit to a dogma expect and demand that all members of their society follow it. Intolerance is widespread and almost taken for granted. Its essential fatuousness is prominently displayed in the ongoing controversy.

None of those who believe in the embryo's right to life are harmed by those who want the right of free choice preserved. The opponents of free choice may justify their intolerance as provoked by the horror of the killing they have to witness: it is the revulsion of deeply offended religious and moral feelings that drives them on. However, one cannot escape the suspicion of hypocrisy since the fervent interest in the embryo often ends with its birth. Children in the United States are more likely to live in poverty and die before their first birthday than are children in other industrial countries. There are 100,000 homeless children in New York alone. Because of budgetary constraints, immunization programs were rejected by the Administration and infants died in epidemics that were preventable.[6] No protest is heard from the conservative groups that fight against free choice.

A nonreligious, moral argument in favor of free choice is cogent. Enforced pregnancy may be looked at as a crime more heinous than rape, in that rape is of limited duration, whereas enforced maternity potentially overshadows an entire life, and often two or even more lives. To be sure, a mother's feelings may change and grow, and the crime of enforced motherhood may lead to bliss and life's fulfillment. But this would not render the crime null and void; rape may give the victim ecstasy, and yet this does not annul the crime—even though some judges are

---

[6]Although President Bush could have stopped the measles epidemic of 1990, he delayed granting the means under various subterfuges and, therefore, was responsible for the consequent death of infants. I am opposed to negative campaigning and, therefore, would not have advised the opposing party in the election to televise President Bush's picture surrounded by dead infants, but many believers may predict that he will have to stare at them for an awfully long time after his demise, which will not take him straight to Heaven.

obtuse enough to believe that it does. It stands to reason that a pregnancy should be repudiated when it is endured against the future mother's will and inner conviction. When a pregnancy leads to giving birth with an unwilling heart and ends in motherhood submitted to only in order to escape the punishment or disgrace sanctioned by churches or the pressures exerted by society, then it is irreconcilable with ethics and is immoral.

Discussions of the abortion controversy (see Thompson, 1971, 1973; Finnis, 1973) are refined and sophisticated, each party adhering to its own style of logical deduction. Such exchanges are "literally interminable," as Posner (1990, p. 129) remarked. Evidently neither logical analysis nor appeal to tradition, ethics and religion leads to a final conclusion that would be satisfactory to both camps. It is, of course, awkward when one party preaches an action to be an intolerable offense, a mortal sin, under all circumstances, and the other declares it to be permissible, even advisable, if certain frequently occurring conditions are present.

In a democracy, one might expect, when respected representatives of morality are in dispute about the right to act in a way that does not damage the rights of other citizens, the State would leave it to the individual to decide which position to support. But this has not been the case. The last government took strong measures against the free-choice movement, even endangering free speech by prohibiting mention of abortion in government supported clinics mandated to advise some 4,000,000 clients on family planning.[7] Foreign countries lost U.S. aid when they took

---

[7]To anticipate a theme to be developed in what follows, the outraged defender of civil liberties may learn from the presiding Justice of the Supreme Court himself how to circumvent rulings and carry dissent to victory. When the Justice

measures to regulate propagation. The U.S. government was assisted in its fight by aggressive private organizations that are allied with politically conservative groups.[8]

The right-to-life movement is coercive in its very foundation and this alone leads to a degradation of women to appliances of propagation, a degradation that has to be banished to the past.

III

The destructive acts, the demagoguery, and above all, the attempt of the anti-choice groups to degrade the standing of women by returning to the days prior to 1973 can possibly be combated with the traditional means of political education, enlightenment, and public indoctrination. A far more formidable opponent is the Catholic Church, whose power and momentous weapons make her appear invincible. She is ready to use her full force to exorcise the evil spirit of freedom when it goes so far as to provide females with the right to make their own decisions about maternity.

---

acknowledged that prayer in school is unconstitutional, he suggested silent prayers. Thus, although the Court approved the ruling that no advice on abortion may be given at the family planning clinics, it can be easily overridden by negative counsel—the clients being told that the clinics are forbidden to tell them that an abortion clinic is located in the next block—or by a private meeting, at which, when off-duty, clinic personnel may give all the requested information.

[8]The Right to Life group has not abstained from inducing corporations, under the threat of boycott, to discontinue their contributions to organizations like Planned Parenthood. "Demonstrations" and protests at abortion clinics, sometimes violent, are not unusual. In some areas, a vociferous minority is so successful in harassing those who perform abortion that women meet increasingly severe obstacles when they want to obtain interventions.

Bishop Leo T. Maher (1916–1991), the head of the Roman Catholic Diocese of San Diego, California, barred Assemblywoman Lucy Killea from communion because she supported the right to abortion, a position which he pronounced to be a grave scandal from the Church's standpoint. With this ruling a priest committed a shocking offense, to which a democratic body politic, in turn, has every right to take strong exception. An elected political representative has the duty to be guided only by considerations of law and welfare of the community, without regard to race or creed. What the Bishop demanded was that the representative give preference to her religious obligation and disregard the welfare of the populace as she gauged it. The Church thus interfered with a citizen's sworn duty. Other ecclesiastical dignitaries have also intimated, or declared openly, that they have the right and duty to deny sacraments to supporters of free choice. This *de facto* policy of the Church renders Catholicism incompatible with the basic principles of a democratic republic. It follows that Catholic legislators and judges in the United States would have the duty to declare a state of conflict of interest when they are called upon to make decisions affecting abortion. If the Church declares a vote in favor of interruption to be a mortal sin, does an abstention from voting on that matter fall into the same category? Can a Catholic entrusted with a public function regarding the common weal be obliged to do the maximum in preventing abortion under all circumstances?

In earlier times, when two contending parties faced each other uncompromisingly, an ordeal revealed the *iudicuum Dei*, God's decision. Modern man has abolished the ordeals of battle, fire, water and whatnot. Still, if not a sparrow will fall without the Father's will, can an election be won without the Lord's blessing? What other conclusion can the staunch believer draw but that the controversy between the Bishop and the Assemblywoman should be decided by that modern ordeal in which the Lord's opinion reveals itself? As it turned out, the *iudicuum Dei* disowned Bishop Maher: the Democratic Assemblywoman Killea was elected State Senator in a predominantly Republican voting district. Believers who are in favor of abortion may take courage from this outcome.[9]

Of course, the enmity of the Catholic Church extends not just to abortion but to any form of family planning. In some countries, this contributes to abysmal social conditions and provokes resistance. Alberto Fujimori, President of Peru, stood his ground against the Church, which opposed his program of family planning, and asserted that the population knew how to distinguish between religious and social affairs (*The New York Times*, November 16, 1990): "We don't want a country populated by children feeding themselves from garbage dumps." For a substantial part of the world's population it may indeed be a

---

[9]The petition of right-to-life groups that the Pope excommunicate two dozen prominent lawmakers who support abortion is a renewed sign of that movement's malice. His Holiness plans to reject the pious appeal. It is almost a betrayal of citizenship to ask the Pope to prevent elected representatives from fulfilling their sworn duty, and it is unbelievably cruel for a Catholic to request that one of his brothers be consigned to eternal perdition.

The Church's readiness to excommunicate lawmakers who favor abortion is in contrast to her attitudes during the dark years of National Socialist oppression. Mortal sins were committed, including the imprisonment and torture of priests, not to speak of the crimes of genocide, but history records no leader, henchman or other adherent of that movement ever being threatened with excommunication.

choice between birth control and children feeding from garbage dumps. The question forces itself upon the mind: Would Jesus prefer children, before their end in starvation, to go through the agony of eating from garbage dumps, or would he prefer their early dissolution in a nirvana that spares them from such suffering?

The artillery at the feminist movement's disposal is not as heavy as the Church's. The defeat of the Pope in Poland, which refused to abolish free choice, in no way assures that Catholicism has lost its hold on the Western mind. It is almost certain that ultimately the Church will succeed in Poland, as it will even in countries with a weaker Catholic tradition. Since the free-choice movement speaks without the authority of a church, it is often forced on the defensive and therefore must raise a shrill, combative voice.

IV

Yet, however strong the enemies of women's right to interrupt, free choice of motherhood must become an inalienable right, as deeply anchored in the national conscience as free speech, immune to interference by government or church. This right must be protected against assault by an immoral minority (I hope it is a minority). The immorality is patent since it is determined to overrule inviolate standards of human existence.

What strategy should be adopted to protect that right? The mass of women voters (there are more female than male voters) is a great power; it has a voice that may penetrate deeper into the heart of the nation than threats of hellfire or the pale abstractions of jurists who have lost contact with live, social reality.

Still, apart from devout women who are unflinchingly tied to opposition by their church affiliations, there are many who for other reasons are not in favor of the right to interrupt. The free-choice movement was forced to be combative and aggressive in its fight for freedom; it has acquired the false reputation in some circles of objecting to women's giving birth. The movement has to disabuse itself of that allegation and substantiate its rejection of any form of coercion. The first aim would be to convince those women who object to freedom of choice for personal reasons that their feelings do not oblige them to deny mercy and empathy to their sisters.[10]

The massive accumulation of arguments in favor of freedom of choice should have a positive effect on the male vote. It is difficult to gauge how many men feel a protest when made aware of discrimination against women. A woman who is seriously engaged in preserving freedom of choice should, one might be justified in assuming, succeed in persuading at least one male voter to cast his vote for a contestant of her choice. Women may have to read Aristophanes's *Lysistrata*, in case of doubt as to how to proceed and learn what those brave Athenians did to end their

[10]In this context the response of American women to Anita Hill's cross examination is pertinent. Whether she spoke the truth or not is not the question; that she was treated by some senators in an irresponsible, arrogant, sadistic, humiliating way as no witness before is unquestionable. One would have expected an uproar against senatorial despotism, an overwhelming rebellion of women against abuse of power. That no senator slapped down those who offended basic democratic rules, and that women's response was less than moderate, are signs that the backlash that was observed in Germany after 1933 has progressed to a frightening degree in this country.

husbands' inane warfare. There is a faint possibility that a renaissance of Women's Lib and its closing ranks with all groups—including conservatives, as long as they are in favor of free choice—might have the result that no one who opposes free choice would have a chance of being elected.[11]

V

One thing is certain: all the opponents of free choice in this country will not be able to deprive women of that right as long as the Supreme Court upholds its 1973 ruling of woman's constitutional right to abortion. It is widely assumed, however, that the majority of Justices feel averse to free choice; this is intimated by the Court's rulings that consistently narrow the range of situations in which abortion is permitted. Thus, the 1973 ruling is gradually being eviscerated. It is possible, even likely, that the Supreme Court will before long decide that the legal status of abortion rests with the States. President Bush, on his first working day in office, called for a Human Life Amendment to the Constitution. All those who earnestly crave the welfare of their country must be prepared for the eventuality of a serious legal attack against the 1973 ruling. As a first step, one has to take a hard look at the courts, and particularly the Supreme Court.

[11]That women are represented by a mere 5 percent of senators and representatives is appalling, a condition that must be speedily corrected.

At the outset, I must remind the reader that within a generation, the Supreme Court has been transformed from the institution led by Chief Justice Warren, which was dedicated to strengthening democratic rights, into what is virtually its opposite. That transformation, started by Richard Nixon, was energized by President Reagan and pursued with equal fervency by his successor. Reagan, who is the personification of America's evil spirit, did his best not only to deprive the U.S. economy of its solid foundation, but also to destroy the country's liberalism, present and future. He was aware that a reactionary President may be followed by a liberal one, whereas Supreme Court Justices, because they are appointed for life, hold their office far longer than a President. He considered, as candidates for the bench, not those who were prominent by knowledge, experience, and wisdom, but primarily those known for their antiliberal, reactionary convictions, not to speak of a bias in favor of enlarging the power of the Executive Branch.

Reagan's appointments, in the view of sober observers, inaugurated a trend which is gradually dissolving the Supreme Court's role in protecting the economically and politically disenfranchised. Justice as a philosophical and legal concept may be undefinable in a broadly acceptable way. But its spirit, that people are treated with dignity and humaneness, cannot long survive in a time when the reactionary ideological commitments of the majority of the court are enforced at the expense of concern for the individual and his rights and social reality.

Reagan's successor followed his path. I shall describe an incident that demonstrates President Bush's tactlessness, insensitivity, and utter lack of fairness, his total disregard of justice in favor of politics. With many candidates to choose from, Bush selected, as a judge for the Federal Appeals Court, a man who had given a tongue-lashing from the bench to some blacks who had protested their own mauling by police dogs: in some societies, the judge said, a person's hand is cut off for thievery, and it may be good for them if they carried around a few scars from the dogs to remind them of their wrongdoing. Far from being shocked, the President apparently took this pronouncement as a recommendation, as evidence of the man's qualification for advancement to an appeals court.

The offensive statement expresses approval of a punitive system current in an Islamic country that imposes sentences that are considered unusual and cruel and prohibited by the U.S. Constitution. Mauling by dogs falls unquestionably into that category. With his ruling the judge also offended the Christian spirit, which is repelled by the idea of permanent disfigurement as testimony to a past misdemeanor. The sign of Cain was meant to protect Cain's life against becoming a victim of the talion principle. With the nomination of a judge who made himself guilty of that outrage, the President participated in the same misconduct. One should keep in mind that the President did not break the law by the nomination, but he committed an act of grave infringement on justice. Indeed, one wonders how a mind inclined to such vulgarity could ever have reached the federal bench.

President Bush's nomination of the mauling-dogs judge proves that his policy was primarily not one of advancing justice but one a racist mentality would find congenial. Was the eagerness to please those who financed his campaign closer to his heart than the common weal? From this choice alone the electorate can derive a fair idea of what Mr. Bush believes American citizens deserve in the way of the administration of justice. The nomination was an encroachment on the basic values in which this country has taken pride. The Senate Judiciary Committee's rejection of the nominee saved the nation from an indelible stigma.

The incident of a judge's approving mauling of blacks by dogs shows the frightening gap between the iniquities a judge will commit without punishment and the demands of justice. Citizens feel protected by Constitution and law, but this is an illusion, as the West Coast Japanese (most of whom were American citizens) found out when they were dispossessed and herded into camps during World War II (Ten Broek, Barnhart, and Watson, 1954). The illegality of this act was at first denied by the Supreme Court, but later acknowledged. Even so, the victims were never commensurately compensated.

It is tragic to notice that human meanness may convert a citizen's existence into one of defenselessness despite "good" laws, which do not provide real protection. Many years ago the Supreme Court ruled that states have the obligation to provide a lawyer for every poor person charged with a serious crime, which certainly is a "good" law. But this constitutional right of poor persons was vitiated by states that kept the pay for lawyers low. "Judges who want to rush death cases through appoint the dregs of the bar. About a quarter of inmates on death row in Kentucky were represented by lawyers who since have been debarred, suspended or convicted of crimes" (Lewis,

1991). The American Bar Association recommended that Congress set minimal standards for defense counsel in capital cases. As could have been predicted, President Bush's Attorney General opposed the bill in the Senate and induced the Senate to reject it.

Final victory in the Reagan-Bush attack on liberalism was achieved when the majority of the Supreme Court became of like mind. Today the nation faces a Court in which a solid majority is rigidly tied to the harshest antiliberal principles. The spirit that dominates that tribunal can best be assessed in its adamant insistence on the death penalty. One has to examine that barbaric infringement on justice and humaneness to recognize what is to be expected from the Court.

VI

Capital punishment is one of American civilization's cankers. Every citizen should be guilt-ridden at the thought that it was ever carried out in his lifetime; yet society at large disregards the outrage and therefore shares the responsibility for officially instituted dehumanization. The dehumanization moves from the sanction of Death Row to the reduction of the defendant to an abstraction. Death row is a revolting abuse of power which man acquires over his victim and which allows him to discharge his sadism without restraint. If the defendant's case finally reaches the Supreme Court, he is reduced to a legal abstraction, no longer a human being but like a skeleton deprived of muscles and organs. At the same time, he has become an important pawn in politics and, in many states, even an asset to governors, who gain in popularity by resisting appeals for clemency. Although among civilized nations the talion principle has been dismissed as a norm for the legal system, thinking in most of the states is still archaic in the extreme when capital crimes are at issue.

The arguments usually raised in favor of capital punishment are all too well known. Its alleged deterrent effect is used as a rationalization. Prior to March 1991, capital punishment was carried out in 13,770 cases. The crime rate quite probably would not have been significantly changed if the defendants had been sentenced to lifelong prison terms. But it stands to reason that prohibition of the sale of arms during that period would have had a more marked effect than capital punishment. In a seminal paper Martha Grace Duncan (1991) maintains that there is a bond between society and criminals, despite the official disapprobation and prosecution. She speaks of our admiration for criminals and uncovers society's need to foster criminality. This has to be considered in trying to understand Congress's continuous refusal to squelch the sources of criminal behavior, one of which is the ready access to an arsenal of weapons. The insistence of legislators on upholding the unchecked sale of weapons presents a provocative sociopsychological problem, for it is a phenomenon demonstrating the covert desire of society to keep crime alive. Not only is reliance on the death penalty disingenuous: by that reliance Congress recommends actions that are—for a variety of reasons—more reprehensible than the crime they purport to prevent. One of those reasons is that the executed person is used as a scapegoat for society's shortcomings. The security of the society at large is made dependent on the extinction of a life, but that life was more frequently than not victimized by nature and nurture; environment and the sentenced person's constitution conspired to form what society considers its dregs. Utterly neglected during his lifetime, after committing a crime the perpetrator becomes the center of society's attention and the victim of the fear that his survival might set a bad example.

To explain why so many people are in favor of the death penalty, one should think of Plato's aphorism that the law-abiding citizen dreams of that which the criminal does. If capital crimes are not followed by the supreme penalty, law-abiding citizens may respond to the vague fear that they might not resist the call of their own murderous impulses.

I used to believe that primitive urges of revenge and the fear of the spread of violent crimes were widely operative. Yet recently it turned out that a large number of people prefer lifelong mandatory imprisonment of murderers to capital punishment. Is it possible that the general feeling about capital punishment has changed more than its adherents are ready to admit? Still, one cannot overlook the sadistic impulse, the morbid excitement, the sensationalism involved. Televising the event would probably excite many.

The death penalty must be abolished, were it only because of the corrosive effect it has on society. Justice William Brennan recognized that the process that leads to Death Row and the lethal events that occur there are not disjoined from the rest of society but recoil on the whole of it. He wrote:

> It is tempting to pretend that minorities on Death Row share a fate in no way connected to our own,

that our treatment of them sounds no echoes beyond the chambers in which they die. Such an illusion is ultimately corrosive, for the reverberations of injustice are not so easily confined. . . . And the way in which we choose those who will die reveals the depth of moral commitment among the living [as quoted in Ingle, 1990, p. 269].

Furthermore, it has been proved that innocents have been executed. Bedau and Radelet (1987) report that between 1905 and 1974, twenty-three defendants were executed for crimes they had not committed (pp. 72–75). Ernest van den Haag considers such hair-raising incidents part of the price for the benefits of capital punishment, which he thinks are substantial. About the executions of innocents, he wrote:

All human activities—building houses, driving a car, playing golf or football—cause innocent people to suffer wrongful death, but we don't give them up because on the whole we feel there's a net gain. Here, a net gain in justice is being done [as quoted in Bedau and Radelet, 1987, p. 23].

Do the Justices agree with van den Haag's warped syllogism? In their statistics, Bedau and Radelet did not take into account mental disease, low intelligence, juvenile age, or other conditions that should have made offenders ineligible for the death penalty. What extent of miscarriage of justice would their inclusion have unmasked?

Two cases of persons rescued from scheduled execution will help clarify what American society seems to consider acceptable. Ronald Monroe had been facing the prospect of execution for eight years. Indigent, a mentally retarded black man with an IQ of 73 to 77 who had neither a criminal record nor a history of violence, Monroe was sentenced to be executed for stabbing to death a neighbor, Lenore Collins, in 1977, when he was 22. Monroe's mother swears that her son was asleep at home the night the murder occurred.

His conviction rested exclusively on the testimony of Collins's children, 11 and 12 years old, who were eyewitnesses of the deed but whose testimony was questionable. None of the forensic evidence to be expected, such as murder weapon, fingerprints, or matching blood stains, was adduced. According to the defense, the murderer was the victim's estranged husband, the children's stepfather. He had tried to stab his first wife to death, was guilty of another knife attack and had been convicted of killing his common-law wife. He was seen in Mrs. Collins's neighborhood the night she was murdered. In a Michigan prison he confessed to a cell mate that he was the murderer.

The children's testimony was hardly suitable as evidence, in view of their contradictory descriptions of what the assailant was wearing. The stepfather had intimidated the daughter, whom he had sexually abused for years. Most of the evidence incriminating the victim's husband never reached the jury and was withheld from the defendant's counsel.

Two weeks before Monroe was scheduled to die, the Governor of Louisiana commuted the sentence to life in prison without parole or probation. If the firm of Paul, Weiss, Rifkin, Wharton and Garrison had not put all its resources in the service of Monroe's defense, he would have been executed.

Nothing was heard about prosecuting the police officers who had withheld the confession of another man. The Governor did not request a new trial but rather "pardoned" the defendant to lifelong imprisonment. Was the Governor convinced that an innocent black man who had escaped death row should be glad to spend the rest of his life in jail?

The Governor's ability to split hairs would have made Thomas Aquinas envious—he was convinced that Monroe had committed the crime, but that enough doubts had been raised to make execution inadvisable. Apparently there are two types of reasonable doubt: one protects a person against being killed, but the other is not strong enough to keep him out of jail for life.

Before turning to another extreme miscarriage of justice, I remind the reader of Dostoevsky's statement: "Everyone is responsible for whatever happens, wherever and whenever it may take place."[12]

On August 23, 1980, Cheryl Fergeson, a sixteen-year-old schoolgirl, was found dead in the town of Conroe, Texas; she had been raped and then choked to death.[13] The girl had come with her team to Conroe for a volleyball tournament. Clarence Lee Brandley, a black supervisor of the janitors at the local high school, was arrested and indicted for rape and murder. Allegedly a police officer had said to Brandley and one of the white janitors, "One of you two is gonna hang for this. . . . Since you're the nigger, you're elected" (Davies, 1991, p. 23). The first trial ended in a hung jury; in the second trial Brandley was

[12]This extreme moral demand may have appeared unenforceable when Dostoevsky enunciated it, but modern technology appears on the verge of making its realization possible, with the advent of two-way cable television.

[13]I have relied on Nick Davies's *White Lies: Rape, Murder, and Justice Texas Style* (1991) for the details of this case. The book is obligatory reading for anyone professing concern about the survival of American democracy.

sentenced to the electric chair. The Court of Criminal
Appeals rejected the defense's appeal twice. Exhibits
disappeared and were replaced by faked ones in the
hope that the defense would not notice.

At last the Court of Appeals granted a new hearing,
which began on September 21, 1987, with Judge Perry
Pickett presiding. This judge, one of the most senior
judges in Texas, who had been on the bench for 30
years, was an outsider to the case. He was a visiting
judge who had been pulled out of retirement to deal
with this particularly sensitive matter. On November
19, 1987, he presented a 47-page analysis of the case,
which began with these words:

> After ten days of trial, the Court became convinced
> that Clarence Lee Brandley did not receive a fair trial,
> was denied the most basic fundamental rights of due
> process of law, and did not commit the crime for
> which he now resides on death row [Davies, 1991, p.
> 370].

It turned out that the defense's accusations, their
suspicions regarding the participants in the earlier
trials—Judge John Martin, the District Attorney, and
the witnesses—were all too justified. Judge Martin,
Pickett reported, had lied, had held secret meetings
with the D.A. during the trial as well as after the
disappearance of the exhibits; he had been hostile
toward Brandley and other black people in his court.
The D.A. had also lied about the secret meetings in
which he and Judge Martin had rehearsed key rulings
in the defendant's second trial; he had concealed evidence, planned to cover up the disappearance of the
exhibits, and tried to deceive the defense by using
fake exhibits. One witness swore that Judge Martin

and the D.A. had been "leaders of the 'project' to convict Clarence Brandley" (p. 327). The court clerk, too, was a liar. Even though she denied it, it was confirmed that she had committed the obscenity of asking Judge Martin to set the day of Brandley's execution on her birthday so that they could celebrate both events at the same time (p. 363). Judge Pickett called her behavior "a sordid instance where the 'project-like' mentality overbore any sense of justice and decency at the courthouse" (p. 371). The investigating ranger had lied. He had threatened to kill a witness, had concealed a tape recording from the defense, and had kept "a blind focus on Clarence Brandley" (p. 371).

Judge Pickett concluded:

> [T]he color of Clarence Brandley's skin was a substantial factor which pervaded all aspects of the State's capital prosecution against him, and was an impermissible factor which significantly influenced the investigation, trial and post-trial proceedings. The tone of the courtroom, as fostered by the District Attorney's office, the judge and the District Clerk's office, was white against black. . . . The authorities wholly ignored any evidence, or leads to evidence, which might prove inconsistent with their premature conclusion that Brandley had committed the crime. The conclusion is inescapable that the investigation was conducted not to solve the crime, but to convict Brandley [p. 371].

The judge's findings conclude with these damning words:

> In the thirty years this court has presided over matters in the judicial system, no case has presented a

more shocking scenario of the effects of racial prejudice, perjured testimony, witness intimidation, an investigation the outcome of which was predetermined,
and public officials who for whatever motives lost
sight of what is right and just [p. 372].

Despite Judge Pickett's denunciation of those who
had brought Clarence Brandley to death row, the
Court of Criminal Appeals judges remained inactive
until the election primaries were over; then, four
months after the Judge had submitted his findings,
they "announced that both sides in the Brandley case
would have to submit written briefs before they could
make a decision" (p. 379). In November 1988, one
year and eleven days after Judge Pickett had ruled
that Brandley's incarceration was an affront to justice,
and after the judges had been safely reelected, they
finally decided to hold a hearing. This eventually led
to Brandley's being acquitted in December 1989, after
nine years of languishing in prison for a crime he did
not commit.

Many a reader will feel that it was unnecessary to
go into the gruesome details of miscarriage of justice
in Clarence Brandley's case; I believe it is incumbent
upon everyone to be fully informed about it. Judge
Pickett's findings demonstrate that the burden of
proof is on those who maintain that the democratic
process is viable. The final outcome of the trial and
the appeal process changed no one's mind in Brandley's hometown. One man said what the majority
probably thought: that if it was not Brandley, then it
"must a bin some other nigger done it" (p. 372). Judge
Pickett had named two white men as the most likely
suspects (p. 370). They were never arrested. Witnesses who at last found the courage to testify in

favor of Brandley lost their jobs on one pretext or another. Brandley did not receive compensation for his nine years of innocence in jail, and none of the officials who neglected their sworn duties was prosecuted. The treacherous District Attorney was elected judge. Oddly enough, all white townspeople continued to say that they had never noticed any sign of racism in their community. Did any of the Justices, not to speak of the townspeople, ever read Nick Davies's book?

The nation, I believe, owes Davies a debt of gratitude for presenting the tragedy of Clarence Brandley in an exemplary, most readable, way. One cannot forget it and is haunted by it, as one should be. But I am not aware that his publication reached a large number of readers or would have aroused repugnance, protest, horror or any of the affects one might have anticipated in members of a community that professes democratic principles. The full history of the case betrays a shocking institutional corruption. Judge Pickett's revelations did not lead to Brandley's immediate release; instead—and this is extremely loathsome—the Appellate Court, as noted, delayed action in order to secure desired election results. Furthermore, if Judge Pickett had not disregarded the Texas law that makes new evidence inadmissible 30 days after the verdict, the Court Clerk's wish that Brandley should be executed on her birthday would have been fulfilled.

Is Brandley's case atypical or exceptional? Davies's account shows with terrifying clarity what can happen covertly around us.

Other industrialized democracies of the West have abolished the death penalty. Anthony Lewis (1990) called the United States, with its 2,200 prisoners on death row, "the execution capital of the Western world." His editorial amounts to ranking the United States at the bottom of Western civilization. Even South Africa has suspended the death penalty. But our country, with its executions of the mentally defective, brain damaged, and juveniles and with the ineffectual representation of destitute condemned persons, who overwhelmingly are blacks, should never give vent to the arrogance of recommending itself as an example worthy of imitation.

When I now compare death row with the concentration camps the Germans instituted for the extermination of the Jews and other minorities, it will be objected that in the concentration camps innocents were killed, whereas those who are held on death row are guilty of a crime. But is the torture of the guilty less reprehensible than that of the innocent? The nation knows of the execrable treatment of death-row inmates and their ending on the electric chair; yet it does not respond but refuses empathy and compassion, just as the Germans did with their death camps.

The fact that the majority on death row are black people is an execrable stigma on society. But there is no end to selective injustice. As I have noted, since almost all of these defendants are indigent, they are represented by court-appointed lawyers who are, to say the least, inexperienced in capital cases. If this were not handicap enough, the lawyer for the appeal has a hard time investigating the alibi, which has often been neglected by his predecessor; he has far fewer means at his disposal than the State; and the higher courts are more inclined to believe the evidence brought forth in the first trial.

The death penalty deserves more extensive discussion than space allows. I shall return to comments on the present Supreme Court, but before doing so I may be pardoned for a personal remark. There is a good chance that the Chief Justice will enrich the Anglo-Saxon vocabulary and that the term Rehnquisition will become current to denote the inequities and abuses in his Court.

VII

It is Chief Justice Rehnquist who has succeeded in leading the Court's majority back to a regressive, harsh disregard for civil rights and a merciless disrespect for human life. Rehnquist, as reported, is ready to admit enforced confessions as evidence, calling the method of obtaining them "harmless error." This will encourage the gradual degeneration of pre-trial examination to the lowest level of the third degree. Even when he was a Supreme Court clerk, Rehnquist had recommended the harmless-error rule, showing that from the beginning of his career he was oblivious of the meaning and necessity of civil rights. The Miranda rule can expect only a limited period of existence.

After 19 years of Rehnquist's urging and planning, the Supreme Court has made itself unavailable to hear second or successive petitions in writs of habeas corpus from prisoners under state death sentences. In 1991 the Court refused to hear the habeas corpus petition of a prisoner under death sentence because his lawyer was three days late in his appeal—a delay beyond his control. One sometimes labors under the illusion that Kafka reached the most profound awareness of our culture's irrationality. Even he would have feared being accused of using a cheap device unworthy of his art if he had let a protagonist say: "I am sorry I have to electrocute your client, whether he deserves it or not, but you are three days late with your petition."

Whatever Kafka's ominous feelings about society may have been, for sure the framers of the Constitution would have preferred the prospect of the Egyptian plagues descending one day on their country to even the possibility that a Justice of the court they created would ever plunge into such an unspeakable outrage. The Rehnquist court decided that a client should be held accountable for his lawyer's failings and that "the petitioner must bear the risk of attorney error" (Epstein, 1991). Do the Justices believe that a black man on death row is given a leave of absence so he can confer with various lawyers and pick the one who seems the most trustworthy? If a Justice decides that an error made by an attorney has earned the death penalty for his client, then Rehnquist must have enough of a sense of humor to grant the rejected petitioner the permission to sue his lawyer for malpractice.

Rehnquist rationalizes his inhumanity by reference to the past, when the defense split claims of petition and prolonged in that way the life of the sentenced person. Is that a mockery of the criminal justice system, as the Chief Justice claims? Is it not rather a mockery of the system when a defendant is executed in one state for a crime that, if he had committed it a few miles away in a neighboring state, would have earned him no more than a few years' imprisonment? Is it not a mockery of the Constitution that the majority denies, against all evidence, that death row and capital punishment are unusual and cruel punishments and therefore prohibited by the Eighth Amendment?

The McClosky case will serve as an example of a flagrant miscarriage of justice that was arbitrary and inexcusable. The defendant was one of four who were involved in an attempted robbery, in the course of which a police officer was killed. The death sentence was passed mainly on the basis of testimony presented by the defendant's cellmate. He alleged that McClosky had confessed his guilt to him. Only after the sentence was imposed did the defense find out that the witness was a police informer who had been promised reduction of his sentence if he produced incriminating evidence against McClosky. Neither defense nor jury was informed of that background. Two jurors declared that if they had known of it, they would never have agreed to a death sentence.

This was a clear instance of the need for a new trial. The defense had to invoke the Freedom of Information Act in order to discover that the testimony was tainted. The Supreme Court decided that the illegality of the testimony should have been raised in the first petition. The director of the Center for Human Rights said: "Ten years ago the idea that we would execute someone in violation of the Constitution was so abhorrent no one could imagine it happening. Now as a result of the Rehnquist Court, what we're seeing and what we are going to see in case after case is people going to the execution chamber in cases in which the jury did not know fundamental things about the case" (Lewis, 1990). Here a grievous breach of the Constitution besmirched the honor of the High Court.

Beside demonstrating the arbitrariness of the Court, this case also illustrates the degradation of human life to an abstraction. The Court's interest is directed, not primarily toward the person but toward a legal phantasmagoria of technicalities and sophistries. It is remarkable with what ease the Court exonerated the state by calling an enforced confession a harmless error, an ease that vanishes when the defense deviates by a triviality from the Court's regulations.

These defects in the court system amount to an alarming, well-documented neglect, prejudice and injustice to which predominantly black death-row inmates are exposed. It is, therefore, cause for the most serious concern when Justice Scalia says he will not automatically grant extension of death penalty appeals beyond the 90 days enforced by law. Some states do not pay lawyers' fees when the appeal court is outside the State. How many lawyers are ready to represent a case before the Supreme Court *pro bono publico*? But at least justice is even-handed: the wretched are treated as cruelly on death row as in the Supreme Court.

It not only sounds like, but is, mockery and insult when the Justice says: "There is even greater need to reject such an automatic rule [of extension] in capital cases than there is elsewhere, since no lawyer should be burdened with the knowledge that if he were only to withdraw from the case, his client's appeal could be lengthened and the execution of sentence, in all likelihood, deferred" (*The New York Times*, February 22, 1991). I am sure lawyers will appreciate the Justice's concern for their peace of mind. They will have less appreciation for Chief Justice Rehnquist's urging a swifter legal process for execution in federal courts. In all seriousness he claims that a system that allows delays in carrying out the death penalty "verges on the chaotic." No doubt, the conspiracy against minorities extends to the ranks of the Supreme Court.

Before Rehnquisition became the fashion of the Supreme Court, it happened that a Justice protested. Justice Harry Blackmun wrote: "This Court must do more than wring its hands when a State uses improper legal standards to select juries in capital cases and permits prosecutors to pervert the adversary process. I therefore dissent" (Ingle, 1990, p. 261). Justice Blackmun dissented because he was certain that Willie Darden "did not have a trial that was fair. . . . I would not allow him to go to his death until he has been convicted at a fair trial" (p. 261). The convicted man was executed on March 18, 1988, without a fair trial. It is highly probable, even almost certain, that he was innocent (Ingle, 1990, p. 254 ff.).

One of those abhorrent features of the Rehnquisition is the sanction of the death penalty for the mentally retarded and psychotic. Can it ever be justified that a person with an IQ of 66 can plead guilty, waive the right to a jury, and be sentenced to die? A person with such reduced mental capacity cannot possibly understand the meaning or consequences of each single process, which makes a travesty out of the court procedure. For one thing, he can be made to confess to crimes he never committed. Functioning as a psychiatrist in a training camp during World War II, I demonstrated this to an incredulous army legal officer. A mentally retarded trainee was accused of having amputated his finger in order to be discharged from army service. Within ten minutes I made the soldier confess in tears that he had killed his grandmother.

The day before his death, one of these unjustly executed prisoners asked: "If I am good, can I wear whatever I want to my funeral?" At the risk of repetition, it should be stated that those who are damaged by low mentality and were victims of neglect from infancy on cannot and should not be held responsible for their crimes and misdemeanors. However, when one reads such exquisite nonsense as that inmates of death row have to suffer the death penalty when their lawyers' errors violate the court's ground rules for considering appeals, one starts to wonder if perhaps mental deficiency is, after all, an infectious disorder.

The moral felonies committed in the spirit of Rehnquisition are best summarized in Ronald Dworkin's words:

> In its recent decisions the Supreme Court (which now seems safely in the hands of justices whom conservatives regard as politically correct) has repealed or undercut traditional constitutional rights in major respects. It has adopted new rules that sharply limit the number of times people sentenced to death can ask federal courts to look at fresh evidence or new arguments. It has decided that it may be merely "harmless error" for police to beat a confession out of a criminal defendant. It has rejected the use of plainly pertinent statistics in deciding whether race has played any role in a decision to execute a black defendant. It has granted states the power to restrict abortions in ways

particularly harmful to poor women, and, most recently, in *Rust v. Sullivan*, it has approved as constitutional an executive order forbidding doctors in any
clinic financed with federal funds to discuss or offer
information about abortion, or to indicate where such
information might be available, even for women who
specifically ask to discuss abortion and have no other
access to medical service [Dworkin, 1991, p. 23].

It can no longer be denied—the feared event has
taken place: the Constitution has been mortally injured and is dying a slow but certain, agonizing
death. The country needs another Paul Revere, this
time one who will call the citizens to active resistance
against the tyranny of Justices who have decided that
the meaning of that document should be made impo-
tent and who have the power to do so.

Coming generations will look at the electric chair
and hear about the pre-execution rituals the way we
look upon the torture chambers and their instruments
that were used in previous centuries. To execute innocent, insane, mentally defective people is a foul
crime, far worse than any the most depraved criminal
can carry out. It is a truism when I point out that the
execution is the consequence of calm deliberation by
people who belong to the elite, most of whom have
profited from exceptional advantages. It is again a
truism that in large measure the crimes the Justices
have to judge were committed by the abused and
neglected victims of nature as well as of society. They
had not been given a chance of developing minimal
barriers against their impulsiveness. Christians
should know, one would think, that the killer deserves more pity and compassion than the killed. But
the Supreme Court declared that neither juvenile age

at the time the crime is committed nor mental retardation are constitutional barriers to execution.

Some enlightened Justices repeatedly and consistently declared that the abolition of the death penalty is mandatory, since the Eighth Amendment prohibits unusual and cruel punishment. A mind may be ever so erudite, knowledgeable and wise, but it will never be able to prove that life on death row and capital punishment are not unusual and cruel. Given the Eighth Amendment, it is an unsolvable enigma how the Supreme Court in 1976 could rule that the death penalty was not inherently in violation of the Constitution.

Years ago a convict who had been strapped to the chair was not killed because of a mechanical defect. Nevertheless, he was not granted a pardon but had to go again through the same agonizing preparation. McClosky was strapped to the electric chair twice because the first time a delay was granted at the last moment. From whatever angle one views it, the death penalty is unique and cruel. Strangely enough, great care is taken to assure that the convicted cannot commit suicide. In some instances the guards have openly confessed their motive by declaring, "You will not escape us," an unmistakable indication of the sadistic pleasure they gain from legalized killing.

Is suicide a forbidden act? Does society have a right to refuse it? Is such a refusal legally warranted? The atrocity of the death penalty would cause less anguish for most prisoners if death were imposed not on them but by them, that is, if the final act were carried out in the way that is preferable to them. In the denial of suicide the primary sadism hidden in the death penalty becomes apparent.

There is another, surprising aspect. The death penalty is supported by conservatives, who usually are devout Christians and, one must assume, believe in a world yonder. Now, one cannot expect that the Lord would send a sinner who has gone through the agony of the death penalty, to purgatory or hell. One can rest assured that the executed person's soul passes through the pearly gates, which would destroy the punitive aspect of the execution. A life sentence, on the other hand, is a punishment. Christians should never declare death to be a penalty, for that is one of the worst blasphemies.

In all that morass of injustice and cruelty, the pawns of justice may take heart that if there is some truth in Christian mythology, the pitiful victims of legalized killing can be certain that they will never meet anyone in Heaven who supported capital punishment.

The Supreme Court Justices themselves would justify their votes in legal terms. Whether they invoke *stare decisis* or declare that they cannot affirm earlier rulings and must fulfill their oath by a principled search for the original intent of the framers of the Constitution, all these arguments are empty subterfuges. Intimate details of their upbringing, religious beliefs, personal fears and rages that operate inside them are the true driving forces. Perhaps Justices should ask the legally unbiased what unusual and cruel punishment is, before condoning the death penalty. This nation will enter the third millennium after the Lord's son let Himself be crucified for the redemption of mankind soiled with the blood of the sick and the wretched.

VIII

I now raise the question again: Was the Morgan custody case and the way it was dealt with by Judge Dixon exceptional or symptomatic? One may conclude, in view of developments since then, that it was symptomatic. Judge Dixon's lack of concern about the mother's rights and individuality, his determination to impress on child and mother his will and to treat them as if they were abstractions, in disregard of individual facets, all are emblematic of what since then has become the spirit of the country.

The principle of equating individuals, in this instance mother and child, with abstractions amounted to a deprivation of the mother's constitutional right to due process and to the overruling of necessities bound to a live reality in favor of the dead letters of a legality inimical to the welfare and growth of life. The Supreme Court, in denying a petition because of a delay of three days, was driven by the same spirit that infused Judge Dixon's rulings. Both courts interpret the law without dignity, kindness, and humaneness. The absence of these qualities makes courts the cemeteries of society.

What should one expect from a Supreme Court that is callous and dehumanizes human beings when it has to rule on the interruption of pregnancy? In the course of time, the Justices' subjective, abstruse, legalistic conceptualizations will win the day. The upshot undoubtedly will be that women's dignity and welfare will be thrown back to the policies and vagaries of state legislatures, as happened to capital punishment, which is the rule in some states and never carried out in others. This must be prevented at all costs.

The rulings of the Supreme Court have, for most people, a religious, awe-inspiring ring; absolute authority is extended to that institution. Yet the framers of the Constitution were wise enough to endow that body with only a fraction of the power it holds now.

Article III, Section 2, of the Constitution defines two classes of cases that may be heard by the Supreme Court: (1) those in which the State is a party, and (2) those which affect ambassadors, other public ministers and consuls—period. Legal minds passionately interested in the survival of democracy in our republic will have to examine how the limits the framers of the Constitution placed on the Supreme Court's power can be used as an antidote to the poison it currently disseminates. It seems to the legally untrained that what was delegated by a simple majority can be taken back by a simple majority. It would not require the complexities of a constitutional amendment but no more than a vigorous attempt on Capitol Hill to end the present nightmare. Once the High Court's power is reduced to its constitutional confines, Congress would have a free hand in introducing laws that guarantee the individual's basic rights. The nation cannot be expected to watch idly while a judiciary limited in judgment by religious dogmata and reactionary prejudices gnaws away piece by piece at what previous Justices, enlightened and humane, have made integral elements of civil and political life. Rehnquisition must end. The gift to women of a life worth living must be preserved.

This scenario will no doubt be called a pipe dream. However, history is not without glorious examples of institutions endowed with vastly greater power than the Supreme Court ever possessed that were defeated nevertheless by powers vastly weaker than the United States electorate. What is necessary is that Congress awaken from its lethargy, which can be easily achieved. Everyone knows that the nightmare of representatives and senators is not being reelected. Every woman knows what to do.

IX

Very clearly, personal feelings have entered the preceding discussion of freedom of choice and the death penalty. They are strange bedfellows: one, the right to end potential human life while in the process of its formation; the other, protection of a human against a premature termination. Yet the way society deals with them is the best barometer of its moral standing.

* * * * *

When contrasted to the grave issues on the national level of freedom of choice and the death penalty, the injustices Morgan had to suffer appear small, but they are emblematic. Her case, too, is a matter of judicial institutions. It should be guaranteed by law that in all cases of custody the present and future welfare of the child is the irreducible principle that has to govern a court's rulings, to the exclusion of other considerations. But precious little is heard in general from the bench about that aspect. The present legal system is evidently not primarily geared to the child's health and welfare. It does not realize that in custody cases the rights of parents, if they are to be considered at all, have to take a secondary place when confronted with the child's well-being (cf. Goldstein, Freud, and Solnit 1973, 1979), which comprises health and development. To be sure, these standards, even while they have to be kept uppermost in sight and mind, cannot always be defined and established with ease; what appears to serve the child's best interest in the present may not be regarded as the optimum a few years from now. A decision is easily found when it concerns a child's physical health; but in the field of mental health it is difficult to determine what constitutes the optimal present that would assure a child's future health of mind. In view of the uncertainty of what demands the child will have to face in the future, it will occasionally be easier to decide in the present which array of circumstances would in all probability be the *least* detrimental.

Let me illustrate the frightening degree of leeway a judge has in disregarding the child's welfare. A mother who was breast-feeding her infant baby was coerced into surrendering it for eight hours once a week to the father, from whom she was separated. Another instance can be learned from a report in the *New York Times* of July 5, 1989. A female judge presided over a custody case similar to Dr. Morgan's, with the exception that it was the ten-year-old daughter who accused the father of incest. Despite this accusation, the judge granted half-year custody to the father and is supposed to have said that the daughter "has learned she can say 'no' to sexual abuse if the father initiates such activity." One can only hope that the report is untrue; otherwise the incident would be an outrage. In any event, judicial arbitrariness and extravagance are to be curbed in all minutiae of family life.

There is an ironic combination of details in the Morgan-Foretich custody case that I do not want to ignore. As mentioned earlier, in 1986 Judge Dixon appointed attorney Linda Holman as a guardian of Hilary's interest *ad litem*. In opposing unsupervised visitation on the grounds that the child's mental health was in jeopardy, she asked repeatedly for a court-appointed, multidisciplinary sex-abuse evaluation of the child and her parents. Morgan supported, and Foretich opposed, the motion. Later he expressed a wish for a team of experts to evaluate the situation and went so far as to state that if a psychiatrist decided it would be in his daughter's best interest if he gave up visitation, he would abide by that decision. Even more puzzling than his original opposition to Holman's motion is Judge Dixon's refusal to provide the evaluation requested by the guardian he himself had appointed. It stands to reason that the distressing situation actually cried out for such an exploration. Since the Judge did not accept the testimony of expert witnesses that had been submitted, it would have behooved him to appoint his own team. It borders on folly when a judge prefers to let a mother smart in jail for 25 months, rather than listen to the findings of experts.

When I recommend the expert as a suitable substitute for a judge in custody cases, the expert must not be regarded as an authority that pronounces a solution once and for all. The needs of children change with their development, and decisions on custody ought to be reviewed periodically. Oddly enough, the narrative of the Morgan case contains only an example of the limitations to which psychiatric experts are subjected, as can be observed in Benedek on the witness stand. The possible shortcomings of experts, however, do not necessarily cause harm; expert witnesses are never in the position of the unassailable authority that Judge Dixon assumed for himself. They have to submit to cross-examination, where prejudices and negligences can be brought out into the open.

What would have been the right way to proceed in a case as complex as that of Hilary—"right" conceptualized here as being in disregard of any limitations imposed by legal abstractions, in pursuit of nothing but the child's interest? Even if worry about the future is dismissed and attention is concentrated exclusively on the present, Hilary's best interest is not easily defined. A child's mental and emotional health is endangered when the parental conflict takes on a proportion that excludes any sort of compromise. If both sides were right, that is, if the father had sexually abused the child and the mother was perverse and insane, as the father claims, there would be no other resort but to have the child raised in a different family, both parents having only the right to supervised visitation. But since there is no conclusive evidence and only suspicion of abuse and no suspicion of maternal perversion or insanity, the necessity and reasonableness of a foster home do not present themselves. Again, it may be futile under these circumstances to ask for the child's *best* interest, and more practicable to search for a solution that will harm the child the least.

The next step would be an estimate of the damage done to the child. The child's play with the dolls reveals a disturbed relationship to the father, a disturbance that is independent of whether the father actually has seduced the child. Hilary herself vigorously opposed being left with her father. When a child protests being left alone with her father with vehemence, this has to be respected; coercion under such circumstances can only be traumatic. That vehemence alone should have made Judge Dixon rule in favor of the father's supervised visitation for the time being.

If Holman's motion had been accepted, the child's future could have been protected with greater ease than after a prolonged period of underground existence, which may have introduced a new traumatic dimension. On the other hand, as discussed before, if the child had stayed with her mother, potentially traumatic conditions such as genital tests, cross-examinations and an overall atmosphere of hostility would have persisted. Oddly enough, these conditions make it feasible that the girl's separation from her mother may have been the lesser of two evils. Some children develop into active, undefeatable adults despite severe traumatization in their young years. It happens rarely but it happens, and Hilary's parents, despite all divergences, have one thing in common: they are both very stiff-necked people. And if Hilary inherited this quality, it may stand her in good stead.

Dr. Morgan's martyrdom of 759 days was rewarded when, following the passage of the aforementioned bill by Congress, she was finally freed on September 25, 1989. She and her fiancé of three years, Paul Michel, a federal appeals court judge in Washington,

D.C., were married the following December. Because of Judge Dixon's standing order to hand Hilary over to her father, she did not dare to reveal her daughter's whereabouts by joining her. But Dr. Foretich's detectives discovered Hilary on February 23, 1990, in New Zealand, and thus the child's odyssey of two-and-a-half years was officially ended. Her maternal grandparents had fled with her to Virginia and then to Nassau, Toronto, Vancouver, Scotland, England and, finally, New Zealand. By her teachers she has been described as happy, well-adjusted and well-balanced.

Dr. Foretich flew to New Zealand and, after a brief supervised visit with Hilary, returned to the United States. Morgan, of course, flew to New Zealand as soon as her passport was released. She has been granted permanent residence in New Zealand and will continue her work there. New Zealand's Family Court has awarded temporary custody of Hilary to the grandparents and appointed an attorney and a child psychiatrist to represent and assess Hilary's best interests. A court will hold hearings to consider Hilary's future. Dr. Foretich wants her returned to the District of Columbia and has applied for sole custody. New Zealand's prime minister declared the child's welfare must be the paramount consideration in any decision. At last, nerve-racking events have simmered down to tolerable proportions, at least temporarily; there is even hope that a permanent situation of security and quietness will favor an optimal development of a highly traumatized child.[14]

[14]According to *The New York Times* of December 1, 1990, a New Zealand Court's decision gave Dr. Morgan custody of the child. She has to remain in New Zealand, report every six months on Hilary's progress, and must refrain from any further publicity about the case. Dr. Foretich said that he would not pursue the case further. The news release ends with the puzzling statement that the

In conclusion, a few personal remarks may be permitted. First, I want to bring up two points in Hilary's history that I feel should be clarified. According to one report (Fremont, 1990, p. 20), Hilary's first neurotic symptoms appeared when she was nine months old. This would have been in April or May of 1983. The infant would scream for no detectable reason, and her nightmares were more violent than usual in infants of that age. Morgan took these as signs that her child was emotionally disturbed. Overnight visits with the father started only in June. This would mean that the earliest neurotic symptoms were present before paternal sexual abuse was possible, and contradict the history, which is reported almost regularly, that the hysterical behavior started "right after Hilary began spending alternate weekends with her father" (Fremont, 1990, p. 22). This discrepancy might be due to inexact reporting. But it must be asked whether seduction is probable at that early age, and what the father could have done to the infant that would result in neurotic symptoms of such intensity as the child showed initially.

The other point that struck me as worthy of further inquiry concerns the father's "visiting the infant several days a week at the home of her baby sitter" (Chin, Sims Podesta, and Kramer, 1989, p. 117) prior to the period of overnight visitations. Was Hilary's life divided from the beginning between two households—the mother's and the baby sitter's? At the age of nine months, the infant apparently had to share three households—mother's, baby sitter's and father's—every other weekend. This alone may put an infant of that age under undue stress.

Judge ruled in Dr. Morgan's favor, "despite reservations about the negative attitudes she has fostered in her daughter."

That much is certain: the exploration of this custody case has led to disquieting insights into the infrastructure of society. A father in a responsible social function, with an impeccable professional record, a respected citizen, has possibly raped his two daughters in childhood; a judge who professes that there is a 50/50 chance of the father's guilt, nevertheless refuses to order supervised visitation of the father and forces the mother into years of prison; the president of a national professional organization is suspected on good grounds of having falsified her testimony in court, and has possibly caused severe damage to one of the contending parties. One has the feeling of being immersed in a quagmire.

That fathers are aroused and attracted by their daughters, usually in prepuberty, puberty and adolescence, is an everyday occurrence and hardly avoidable. Only a very small percentage of them, however, is unable to resist this call of nature; attraction and its mastery will persist in the majority. Why mothers, in contrast to fathers, escape manifest incest has not yet been satisfactorily explained, but it is a fact that incest between mother and son is a rarity. If Foretich really did what his daughters insist he has done, I would not call it an "unnatural" crime; it is a crime against culture, but not nature. The problem is not only why some fathers are overwhelmed by the impulse, but also why not more fathers are victimized by it.

Judge Dixon's rulings strike the layman as a disaster. Many may think, in contrast to the Judge, that the evidence submitted to the Court validated the father's guilt conclusively. The decision of the Fourth U.S. Circuit Court of May 17, 1988, proves that Judge Dixon erred when he decreed the "inadmissibility" of some evidence. But even if some or all of the evidence before him would have had to be ruled inadmissible, there can be no question that a situation of doubt in the father's innocence existed, as confirmed by the Judge's admission of a state of equipoise. After all, if there is a 50/50 chance that a bridge will collapse, no judge would order a defendant to cross it. How Judge Dixon could insist on unsupervised visitation in the presence of equipoise is perplexing. It would be of interest to know his reasoning. It is a loss to the sociology of jurisdiction that he refuses to be interviewed. I hope he will write his memoirs someday.

The Newsletter of Friends of Elizabeth Morgan of spring 1990 carries a letter from a retired Administrative Judge who calls Judge Dixon's conduct unethical and incompetent. He insists that the case should have been assigned to another judge after the first year, and that the Chief Justice of the Court should not have kept silent. Indeed, many people would have felt reassured of the United States' judicial system if a gesture of that kind had eventuated.

My harsh words about a judge may sound as if I were ignorant of Aristotle's truism that man, when separated from law and justice, is the worst of all animals. However, if it is true that in the District of Columbia a convicted burglar faces an average of 17 months in jail, a drug dealer 16 months, an auto thief 14 months, then I do not know where to look for the worst of animals when I hear that a citizen was kept behind bars for over two years without a trial and sentence. The question has been raised whether the custody case had degenerated into a feud between Dixon and Morgan. I surmise that Morgan was not wise and disciplined enough to show in court the advisable submissiveness, but that she provoked the Judge, who reportedly never lost his temper. But what went on behind the curtain of austerity? Was he fuming because this provocative little fireball did not change her style in the dignified hall of justice? Something must have gone wrong in the judgment of a person who treated evidence that he says is in equipoise as if it did not exist.

Dr. Benedek's offense, which appears to be confirmed, is most disheartening. It affords the inference that no one's uprightness may be trusted unreservedly. Severe action should be taken if the content of Dr. Kleinman's letter is true to fact, which should not be too difficult to find out. Dr. Benedek is said to follow her attorney's advice in not answering questions regarding her testimony. Does this smack of a retreat into a kind of Fifth Amendment defense? The correctness of Dr. Kleinman's letter as well as Dr. Benedek's technique in examining Hilary are legitimate subjects of investigation.

As I stated in the beginning of this essay, there is a puzzling problem left. It is connected with the question: did Dr. Foretich do it or did he not do it? The majority of those directly concerned with the case say the evidence in his disfavor is overwhelming. As noted earlier, if we knew for sure that Foretich did not seduce either daughter, then there would arise the intriguing problem of how it could happen that an innocent man could get so inextricably enmeshed in a net of compromising evidence. I must admit that I personally harbor some doubt about his guilt. I must also admit that I have nothing concrete to put my finger on in order to justify my doubt; but I remind the reader of cases of judicial error, such as mistaken identity and the long list of defendants who were proved guilty by what seemed incontrovertible evidence that later turned out to have been spurious. It is merely a feeling I have, despite the evidence that makes Foretich's guilt highly probable—but not certain, I want to add quickly, without disputing for a moment that the abundance of evidence against Foretich made supervised visitation a matter of common sense and of psychological necessity.

On the other hand, if one feels certain that Dr. Foretich raped his two daughters, other questions have to be answered. Why did he so willingly submit to lie detector tests? Why did he not prevent his father from requesting Jane's examination, which, as he should have known, would reveal his perverted dealings with her? Why does he appear on talk shows, grant interviews, and swear to God that he could never commit such atrocities? Why does he ask to be psychologically examined? If he did it, he should stay away from lie detectors and psychologists. If he had accepted supervised visitation without fanfare, the whole matter would have come to the attention of hardly a few. To be sure, August Aichhorn, as I recall, spoke of a type of delinquent who, despite irrefutable evidence confronting him, denies any misdeed and insists on his innocence, because he is convinced that a miracle will at the last moment save him from humiliation, sentence and jail. As a matter of fact, Judge Dixon acted as a kind of guardian angel in Dr. Foretich's favor and has held a protective hand over him when scores of experts were ready to rush into the courtroom and point an accusing finger at him.

I do not think that Dr. Foretich belongs to the type of delinquent that Aichhorn described. That type is found more frequently among juveniles. My theory is a simple one. He was himself a victim of sexual abuse as an infant, or as a child, or in prepuberty, and has repressed all memory of the trauma or traumata he supposedly had to suffer. As a consequence, according to this theory, he would be forced to do to his children what was done to him, and would do it in a twilight state of mind. He would have as little recollection of having violated his own brood as of having been violated himself, and would rightly rage when anyone is certain of his misdeeds. My suggestion would throw light on his counterproductive behavior, which is one of the intriguing questions in a story abundant in perplexities. There are not many options to explain his actions; early traumatization followed by twilight states is the one possibility.

I cannot express enough my feelings of admiration for Dr. Morgan, and my gratitude. She has been scorned for her narcissism, which necessitates a remark. There is a federal prison, I understand, to which the wealthy who were convicted of fraud are sentenced. I hear that this jail is "hygienic" and not uncomfortable. No such consideration was extended to her. Justice did its best to undermine her morale and she was treated like a thief or prostitute, without a glimmering light at the horizon that would promise a termination of her ordeal in the foreseeable future. It is not easy to write books, be prominent in a medical specialty, appear on talk shows and have the endurance to withstand 759 days of voluntary incarceration under the worst conditions, without a wholesome measure of narcissism.

I spoke of gratitude owed her. Her sacrifice not only saved a child but also aroused attention to the plight of hundreds, if not thousands, of mothers who were treated almost as rudely by the courts as she was; she was bound to earn a nimbus. She reminded some of Joan of Arc; and indeed, while it is true that she did not suffer Joan's physical torture, her anguish was of far longer duration. Time will embellish her image and darken that of her adversary. At any rate, in a time of declining respect for and belief in values, she has given many the uplifting feeling that idealism has not withered away but remains aflame. That her liberation took so long and that no storm of protestation set in earlier make many stand deeply in her debt.

She has borne her suffering magnificently and in an exemplary manner. The certainty of her having a permanent place as an outstanding woman in the annals of the 20th century may console her for 759 days of agony. There will also be a few words said about Judge Dixon.

REFERENCES

Bedau, H. A., & Radelet, M. L. (1987), Miscarriages of justice in potentially capital cases. *Stanford Law Review*, 40:21–179.

Chin, P., Sims Podesta J., & Kramer, L. (1989), Trouble: Vowing to protect her child from rape, Elizabeth Morgan faces her 23rd month in jail. *People Magazine*, June 12, 1989.

Davies, N. (1991), *White Lies. Rape, Murder, and Justice Texas Style*. New York: Pantheon Books.

Duncan, M. G. (1991), A strange liking for criminals. *University of Illinois Law Review*, 1991:1–53.

Dworkin, R. (1991), The Reagan revolution and the Supreme Court. *The New York Review of Books*, July 18, 1991, pp. 23–28.

English, B. (1989), In the best interest of the child? *Boston Globe Magazine*, July 16, 1989.

Epstein, J. G. (1991), Why the High Court is insular. *The New York Times*, September 18, 1991, Op-Ed page.

Finnis, J. (1973), The rights and wrongs of abortion. A reply to Judith Thompson. *Philosophy and Public Affairs*, 2:117–145.

Fremont, C. (1990), The real Elizabeth Morgan story: What the jury was never told. *Moxie Magazine*, 1990, 3rd issue.

Goldstein, J., Freud, A., & Solnit, A. (1973), *Beyond the Best Interest of the Child*. New York: Free Press.

———— ———— (1979), *Before the Best Interest of the Child*. New York: Free Press.

Ingle, J. B. (1990), *Last Rights*. Nashville, TN: Abingdon Press.

Lewis, A. (1990), A rage to kill. *The New York Times*, May 18, 1990, Op-Ed page.

———— (1991), A muted trumpet. *The New York Times*, August 16, 1991, Op-Ed page.

Posner, R. A. (1990), *The Problem of Jurisprudence*. Cambridge, MA & London: Harvard University Press.

Ranke-Heinemann, U. (1990), *Eunuchs for the Kingdom of Heaven. Women, Sexuality and the Catholic Church*, trans. P. Heinegg. New York: Doubleday.

Simon, K. (1982), *Bronx Primitive: Portraits in a Childhood*. New York: Viking Press.

Szegedy-Maszak, M. (1989), Who's the judge? *New York Times Magazine*, May 21, 1989.

Ten Broek, J., Barnhart, E.D., & Watson, F. W. (1954), *Prejudice, War and the Constitution*. Berkeley: University of California Press.

Thompson, J. (1971), A defense of abortion. *Philosophy and Public Affairs*, 1:47–66.

———— (1973), Rights and deaths. *Philosophy and Public Affairs*, 2:146–159.

C. G. Jung, a Witness or, the Unreliability of Memories[1]

Our understanding of those who contributed extraordinary values to our culture is the least advanced of the many topics of psychology. The sequence of events in the lives of geniuses is usually well known, but, as is often the case in biographies, their sexual lives remain obscure. It is true that the sexual lives of some geniuses have been explored—but more often than not, I suspect, for the sake of sensationalism rather than out of serious interest. Since the geniuses who receive that attention are well known, the general public tends to follow such reports with particular eagerness. The reader's response depends partly on when the genius lived: the earlier that period, the less critical and more liberal the reader's reaction. Sophocles's sexual life would hardly arouse a ripple today.

I do not intend to pursue the history and meaning of the public's reception of reports about the sexual lives of great men. This essay takes as its starting point a controversy about an alleged sexual episode

---

[1]In part, this essay incorporates, in condensed form, a German publication (Eissler, 1982) on the psychological aspects of the Freud-Jung correspondence.

in the life of Sigmund Freud (1856–1939), more precisely, the rumor surrounding his relationship to Minna Bernays (1865–1941), the younger sister of his wife, Martha Bernays (1861–1951). The possibility that Freud and Minna had an intimate relationship has been discussed off and on. The history of that rumor is not without interest and consequence. But first a few words about Minna Bernays.

She became engaged to Ignaz Schönberg (1856–1886), a Sanskrit scholar and close friend of Freud's. The two sisters and their fiancés formed a close-knit group. After Schönberg broke off the engagement in 1884—because he suffered from tuberculosis—and shortly thereafter died, Minna Bernays never fell in love again, so far as is known. Freud took on the role of an older brother who felt responsible for her welfare. After the birth of Freud's last child, Minna Bernays became a permanent member of the Freud household, moving in with them in 1896. She shared domestic duties with her sister and actively helped to bring up her three nephews and three nieces. Allegedly Freud said that she was one of the only two people who believed in him during the pioneering years of his splendid isolation (see Gay, 1988, p. 76n.). She was, no doubt, intellectually closer to Freud than Martha was. Not an attractive woman, she was witty, outspoken in her criticism, well educated and interested in many subjects.

She accompanied Freud on trips when his wife was not able to do so, which gave rise to the rumor of an intimate relationship. Freud was aware of this. Eva Rosenfeld, who was in analysis with Freud and moved in his circle, told me in an interview that Freud expressed surprise that she never brought up, in her treatment, the rumor she must have heard about him and his sister-in-law.

The earliest published reference to that rumor is in Ernest Jones's Freud biography. He wrote:

> She [Minna Bernays] and Freud got on excellently together. There was no sexual attraction on either side, but he found her a stimulating and amusing companion and would occasionally make short holiday excursions with her when his wife was not free to travel. All this has given rise to the malicious and entirely untrue legend that she displaced his wife in his affections. Freud always enjoyed the society of intellectual and rather masculine women, of whom there was a series in his acquaintanceship [Jones, 1953, p. 153].

Jones's remark did not leave any particular impression. As far as I know, hardly any attention was paid to it in the secondary literature. But in 1969, when Billinsky[2] published an interview he had had with C. G. Jung (1875–1961) in 1957, in which Jung alleged firsthand knowledge of that illicit relationship, the news echoed through the world press. Billinsky's article contains the only documentary evidence, if one can call it that, of an intimate relationship, and it therefore deserves scrutiny. Two points are to be weighed: (1) the accuracy of Billinsky's report, and (2) Jung's reliability in recalling an event that had

[2]According to the obituary in the *Boston Globe* of March 15, 1984, John Billinsky (1917–1984) was born in Philadelphia and educated at the Hartford School of Education, Hartford Theological Seminary, Harvard University, the C. G. Jung Institute in Zurich, and Acadia University in Nova Scotia; he was professor of psychology and clinical studies at Andover Newton Theological School and on the staff of Boston City Hospital from 1945 to 1981.

happened exactly 50 years-less-two-months prior to the interview.

In an introductory remark Billinsky refers to a report in *The New York Times* by which he felt provoked. That article (September 5, 1969) quoted from a letter Freud had written in 1923 to G. Stanley Hall (1846–1924), president of Clark University, where Freud had received an honorary degree in 1909. Freud, the report stated, disagreed with Hall's suggestion that the split between Freud and Jung that developed in 1912 was a classic case of adolescent rebellion. It was not "a case where a father did not let his sons develop, but . . . the sons wished to eliminate their father, as in ancient times" (as quoted in Billinsky, 1969, p. 39). That remark, however, which appears in Freud's letter to Hall of 28 August 1923 (Freud, 1960b, p. 312), was made about Alfred Adler (1870–1937). Freud was critical of Hall's "very definite stand in favor of Alfred Adler." Jung was not mentioned.[3]

As will be discussed, some of the statements that Billinsky attributed to Jung are contradictory, improbable and even bizarre, so much so that I felt certain that the content of the interview was his invention. I was confirmed in that belief by E. A. Bennet, who was a close friend of Jung's and whom I interviewed in London (July 1972). He was certain that Jung had never made the reported statements about Freud and Minna Bernays, if only because he would have made himself guilty of an unpardonable indiscretion by conveying extremely confidential matters to a person

[3]In 1914 Freud complained to Jones that he felt hurt by Hall's having become a follower of Adler (Jones, 1955, p. 58).

contradictory

with whom he was only distantly acquainted and of whose discretion he could not have been certain. I need not dwell on the other reasons Bennet adduced for the interview's fictitious nature, because Dr. Carl Alfred Meier, a friend of Billinsky's, who was Jung's confidant (Jung called him "my best pupil" [Billinsky, 1969, p. 41]) and whose reliability is above doubt, confirmed the substance of Billinsky's report. Jung, Dr. Meier informed me, had given him exactly the same account. Thus, one can feel assured that Billinsky's article is a reliable account of what he had been told by Jung.

The interview took place on May 10, 1957, at 4:30 p.m. in Jung's home in Küsnacht, and was recorded by Billinsky later the same day. I plan to examine, one by one, the evidence for and against Jung's statements as far as they deal with Freud. This will take me at times deep into the biographies of Freud and Jung. A digression into Jung's childhood history will become unavoidable in order to get at the meaning of what he communicated to Billinsky.

I

In meeting with Jung, Billinsky did not have the intention of discussing details of Freud's biography; these came up more or less accidentally. After an hour of relaxed, mutually complimentary conversation about matters of Protestant theology, theological training in the United States, and Jung's Terry Lectures of 1937 on psychology and religion at Yale, Billinsky felt that it was time to leave. When Jung urged him to stay, Billinsky inquired about "how you and

Freud parted ways" (Billinsky, 1969, p 41). Jung replied that when he was working on his monograph *Wandlungen und Symbole der Libido* (later translated as *Psychology of the Unconscious,* Jung, 1916) he "thought that Freud would accept what I had to say. . . . The only thing he saw in my work was 'resistance to the father'—my wish to destroy the father. When I tried to point out to him my reasoning about the libido, his attitude toward me was one of bitterness and rejection" (Billinsky, 1969, p. 41).

The way Freud received Jung's work can be examined objectively, since it is documented extensively by his letters. Freud's earliest response was a positive one. When he received the draft of a lecture that later became part of the *Wandlungen,* he wrote, "I read your essay with pleasure the day it arrived" (19 June 1910[4]). In a letter of 29 August 1911 Jung asked Freud not to be sparing in his criticism and suggested that Freud, when reading the *Wandlungen,* should let it "unleash" his fantasies and associations, and added, "I am sure you will hit upon strange things."

One finds some noteworthy and partly premonitory comments in a letter of 12 November 1911. There Freud wrote, after having read the first part of Jung's paper:

> The reading for my psychology of religion is going slowly. One of the nicest works I have read (again), is that of a well-known author on the "Transformations and Symbols of the Libido." In it many things are so well expressed that they seem to have taken

[4]All letters from the Freud-Jung correspondence referred to in this essay are identified by their dates only, by which they may easily be located in McGuire's text (McGuire, 1974).

on definitive form and in this form impress themselves on the memory. Sometimes I have a feeling
that his horizon has been too narrowed by Christian-
ity. And sometimes he seems to be more above the
material than in it. But it is the best thing this promising author has written, up to now, though he will do
still better. In the section about the two modes of
thought I deplore his wide reading. I should have
liked him to say everything in his own words. Every
thinker has his own jargon and all these translations
are tedious.

Not least, I am delighted by the many points of
agreement with things I have already said or would
like to say [Freud's emphasis].

These words vividly portray the keen, immediate
pleasure Freud took at first contact with the *Wandlungen*. They also contain the first hints of the later
divergence when Jung took religion as part of meta-
physics and Freud took it as part of psychology and
culture.

On 10 January 1912 he called Jung's demonstration
of "unconscious heredity in symbolism," as expli-
cated in the *Wandlungen*, one of the "two recent . . . most significant . . . contributions to [psy-
choanalysis]." This was followed, more than one
month later (29 February 1912), by Freud's assuring
Jung of his "keen interest in your libido paper." Toward the end of the year (14 November 1912), Freud
expressed eagerness to get offprints of the lectures
Jung had given in the United States, because "your
long paper on the libido [the *Wandlungen*], part of
which—not the whole—I liked very much, has not
clarified your innovations for me as I might have
wished." The difference between Freud's and Jung's

theories was great enough to make Freud remark, in the same letter, "You can count on my objectivity and hence on the continuance of our relations; I still hold that personal variations are quite justified and I still feel the same need to continue our collaboration." Earlier, in an undated letter written around 22 June 1910, he had remarked that "despite all its beauty, I think, the essay lacks ultimate clarity. The dream is not pertinently characterized. This indeed is a serious objection."

In discussing Jung's complaint to Billinsky and others about Freud's negative reaction to the *Wandlungen*, one must not neglect the testimony of an eye-witness, Jung's wife, Emma (1882–1955). On 14 November 1911 she wrote to Freud:

> Lately Carl [Jung] has been analysing his attitude to his work and has discovered some resistances to it. I had connected these misgivings about Part II [of the *Wandlungen*] with his constant worry over what you would say about it, etc. It seemed out of the question that he could have resistances to his own work; but now it appears that this fear of your opinion was only a pretext for not going on with the self-analysis which this work in fact means.

Her communication advances the possibility that Jung's complaints to Billinsky were derivatives of his own inner conflicts while producing the *Wandlungen*, for Freud's letters dating from before the break contain sober argumentation, which evidently strove to probe the bottom of their theoretical differences. Jung's answers were not always free of irritation. His letter of 15 November 1912, to name just one such instance, contains reproaches, as if Freud had tried to curtail or do away with his independence. But nothing of the kind can be found in the published correspondence. Freud admitted the possibility of misunderstanding and suggested postponement of all theoretical discussions to the time of a personal meeting. Jung, however, did not heed Freud's request, and this created a somewhat irritated atmosphere until at last, on 24 November 1912, a meeting took place in Munich. Jung's response (26 November 1912) to their meeting sounded as if all their differences had been resolved. He wrote that he had understood Freud for the first time, and went on: "Please forgive the mistakes which I will not try to excuse or extenuate. . . . I am most distressed that I did not gain this insight much earlier. It could have spared you so many disappointments." Freud too was delighted by the turn of events. His impression of the meeting is best described in a letter to Putnam of 28 November 1912 (McGuire, 1974, p. 522): "Everybody was charming to me, including Jung. A talk between us swept away a number of unnecessary personal irritations. I hope for further successful cooperation. Theoretical differences need not interfere. However, I shall hardly be able to accept his modification of the libido theory since all my experience contradicts his position." His answer to Jung, written a day later, likewise expressed his great satisfaction. Two sentences seem particularly noteworthy: "I believe we shall have to lay by a fresh store of benevolence towards one another, for it is easy to see that there will be controversies between us and one always finds it rather irritating when the other party insists on having an opinion of his own." Such a principle should have served well to bridge any future disagreements. About Jung's paper he added:

> I am gradually coming to terms with this paper . . . and I now believe that in it you have brought us a great revelation, though not the one you intended. You seemed to have resolved the riddle of all mysticism, showing it to be based on the symbolic utilization of complexes that have outlived their function.

Jung's answer of 3 December 1912 was a thunderbolt. It contained a complete turnaround. He attacked Freud in the rudest way and made fun of him for the remark just quoted. Yet Freud's antecedent communications contain no relevant provocation. To the contrary, not only Freud's letter written after the Munich meeting but also the preceding ones are noteworthy by reason of the expressions of affection, fondness and attachment they convey; evidently he tried his best to circumnavigate the rocks on which their friendship could be wrecked.

One would think that to find a "great revelation" in a paper is, after all, quite a compliment, even if a reservation is attached to it. There was no ostensible reason for Jung's renewed aggression, unless one assumes that he was unable to tolerate any kind of criticism and demanded exceptionless surrender without discussion or objection. Freud's letters also demonstrate that there was no trace of dogmatic intolerance on his part, nor is there a single reference to a charge of "resistance to the father" or to a "wish to destroy the father." Nor can the bitterness and rejection be discovered that Jung attributed to Freud in the interview.

But Jung went further and challenged Billinsky in a clever way. He remarked that "People still think that *Psychology of the Unconscious* was the reason for my break with Freud" (Billinsky, 1969, p. 41), thus intimating that the *Wandlungen* was not the true cause. This is surprising in the light of his statement two years later in a television interview, according to which, aside from "a *reservatio mentalis*" about "quite a number of his [Freud's] ideas," the publication of the book *Psychology of the Unconscious* was "the real . . . [and] the final cause" (cf. McGuire and Hull, 1977, p. 433). He was not aware that with this statement he disavowed much, if not most, of what he had told Billinsky not so long ago, as the reader will learn presently.

Upon hearing this remark of Jung's, Billinsky naturally was prompted to inquire as to other motives, which Jung readily divulged and which fill the next six paragraphs of the printed interview. I shall not follow their sequence but start with what Jung had to say about Freud and his relationship with his wife.

II

Freud, so Billinsky was told, had made a tactless remark about her when he met Jung and his wife at the hotel upon their arrival in Vienna: "I am sorry," he is alleged to have said, "that I can give you no real hospitality; I have nothing at home but an elderly wife"; at this remark, Jung added, his own wife "looked perturbed and embarrassed" (Billinsky, 1969, p. 42). No one else ever heard Freud make such a disrespectful, indeed vulgar, remark about his wife.

Furthermore, for Freud to have made this remark would have meant that he had suffered a temporary amnesia, for he would have forgotten that he had at home, besides "an elderly wife," six lively, spirited children, aged 12 to 20, and a sister-in-law, whom Jung called, in the course of the interview, very good looking.

What Freud could have meant by "no real hospitality" is likewise puzzling. He had earlier (21 February 1907) written Jung about what to expect at his visit. Freud regretted that Jung did not come at Easter time, when Freud would have had more free time:[5] "I am taken up every day from eight to eight with the occupations known to you." He asked Jung to spend a Sunday with him (Jung did meet Freud on Sunday, March 3, 1907), because then he would be free the whole day. "I further assume," he continued, "that you will be willing to forgo the theatre on the few evenings you will be spending in Vienna [the Jungs stayed a week], and instead to dine with me and my family and spend the rest of the evening with me." He also intended to introduce Jung to the small group of his followers.

This letter would make no one expect an apology for not offering "real hospitality"; on the contrary, it makes it explicit that the whole family was ready to welcome the guest. It is difficult to imagine what Freud could have added to effect real hospitality. It is highly improbable, to say the least, that Freud either made the gross remark about his wife or apologized for deficient hospitality.[6]

---

[5] In Austria, the Easter holidays include Easter Monday as well as Sunday.

[6] Apparently Jung was entertained also during the day by the Freud family, for Martin Freud (1957) reports that Mathilde, Freud's eldest daughter, accompanied Jung on a downtown shopping trip.

Soon thereafter, Jung launched his second attack:

> At Freud's home that evening, during dinner, I tried
> to talk to Freud and his wife about psychoanalysis
> and Freud's activities, but I soon discovered that Mrs.
> Freud knew absolutely nothing about what Freud
> was doing. It was very obvious that there was a very
> superficial relationship between Freud and his wife
> [Billinsky, 1969, p. 42].

Jung refers here to Martha Freud's distance from,
not to say indifference to, psychoanalysis, which
Freud himself acknowledged (1 September 1911):
"[A]s you know, [my wife] is not personally involved
in psychoanalysis." But what Jung erroneously interpreted as signifying a "very superficial relationship"
formed in reality the foundation of their closeness.
For in marital relations of the Victorian era, quite frequently the wife was not to be "degraded" by
involvement in the husband's professional affairs.
Whoever has read Freud's letters to his "little prin-
cess" during their engagement[7] will understand that
nothing was further from his mind than marrying a
woman with whom he might one day discuss libido,
perversions, and the Oedipus complex, subjects that
he himself would have rejected with disgust during
the years of their passionate courtship.

It is instructive to compare Jung's recollection with
that of Martin, Freud's eldest son, who was 18 years
old at the time of Jung's visit:

> The children's contacts with the learned men who
> came to see him [my father] to discuss his theories

[7]That is, those published in Jones (1953) and by Ernest Freud (Freud, S.,
1960a).

were naturally of the slightest. Such visitors were usually asked to stay for a meal and nearly always, we saw, they had little interest in the food they were offered and perhaps less in mother and us children. However, they always worked hard to maintain a polite conversation with their hostess and her children. . . . Nevertheless, it could be seen quite easily that all they wanted was to get this social occasion over and done with and to retreat with father to his study to hear more about psychoanalysis. Jung was an exception. He never made the slightest attempt to make polite conversation with mother or us children but pursued the debate which had been interrupted by the call to dinner. Jung on these occasions did all the talking and father with unconcealed delight did all the listening. There was little we could understand, but I know I found, as did father, his way of outlining a case most fascinating. I can recall today the case of a man who, after being shy and inhibited during the first two-thirds of his life, developed in late middle age a forceful and dominating personality, and the story of another man, a schizophrenic, whose drawing showed an amazing vitality and excellence.

Neither cases had in themselves much importance. Discussed by Jung, they became clear pictures [Freud, M., 1957, p. 108f.].

As will be seen, Jung's unfavorable comments about Martha Freud were not without purpose. They were meant to strengthen his visitor's readiness to believe that a startling event he was in the process of communicating had actually taken place:

Soon I met Freud's wife's younger sister. She was very good-looking and she not only knew enough about psychoanalysis but also about everything that Freud was doing. When, a few days later, I was visiting Freud's laboratory, Freud's sister-in-law asked me if she could talk with me. She was very much bothered by her relationship with Freud and felt guilty about it. From her I learned that Freud was in love with her and that their relationship was indeed very intimate. It was a shocking discovery to me, and even now I can recall the agony I felt at the time [Billinsky, 1969, p. 42].

This event cannot have taken place in the way Jung reported. The mere physical circumstances of Freud's apartment and professional suite suffice to throw doubt on Jung's account. Freud had no laboratory—Jung, however, had one. Since 1896 Freud had occupied three professional rooms on the ground floor (office, study, waiting room) that were separate from his living quarters located one story above. Jung may have recalled these three rooms erroneously as a laboratory. But as we know from Freud's abovementioned letter to Jung, the "laboratory" was occupied from 8 a.m. to 8 p.m. The secret meeting between Jung and Minna Bernays therefore had to have taken place after 8 p.m. Minna Bernays was certainly not in the habit of sauntering through her brother-in-law's office, nor could she have been alone with Jung for any length of time to speak of, either there or in the living quarters. Jung's presence was eagerly sought by Freud or taken up by the family when they met for a meal. If one were to accept Jung's account, one would have to assume that Minna Bernays secretly waited on the landing of the second floor for a moment when Freud left his office, then rushed downstairs in order to catch Jung alone. How long did it take her to pour out her guilt-laden heart to the stranger? She could not have been certain when Freud would return and, therefore, must have left in a hurry.

Invalidating factors of external reality aside, Minna Bernays was 44 years old at the time when she was supposed to have divulged a well-guarded secret that shook her conscience to a stranger 12 years younger than she, to whom she had been introduced only a few days before. And Freud is supposed to have noticed neither Jung's bewilderment when his revered authority, the man he idealized, was suddenly thrown off his pedestal, nor Minna's embarrassment and discomfiture for having betrayed, with her confession, a man to whom she owed loyalty and gratitude for his continuous support, care and many kindnesses. Her alleged behavior, furthermore, does not conform with her personality as described by all observers: reserved, critical, somewhat teacher-like. She was a lady from northern Germany, much concerned with order and manners. Jung was right when he observed that she took a keen interest in Freud's professional affairs, from which Martha kept away. Her brother-in-law's research and plans were an important part of her interests. Therefore, she was bound to know what that visitor of 1907 meant to Freud: the prospect of a basic change in the official standing of his new psychology. Is it likely that at such a critical moment she would have stabbed Freud treacherously in the back and endangered one of his most promising and cherished expectations? I am certain Freud would never have forgiven her for that betrayal. However, no conflict is known to have ever imperiled their friendship, and she continued to live with Freud's wife and unmarried daughter to the last days in London. Thus, we would have to believe that she carried the secret of her disloyalty undisclosed to the grave (except, of course, to Jung), and that Freud had squandered his friendship on a person undeserving of his trust.

If one gives credence to that part of Jung's interview, one would have to explain how it happened that he squared his "agonizing" knowledge with the high praise he conveyed to Freud in his letters after leaving Vienna. On 31 March 1907 he wrote, "I am no longer plagued by doubts as to the rightness of your theory. The last shreds were dispelled by my stay in Vienna"; he speaks of the "tremendous impression" Freud made on him and of "the depths of [his] gratitude and veneration," and adds: "I hope and even dream that we may welcome you in Zürich next summer or autumn. A visit from you would be seventh heaven for me personally; the few hours I was permitted to spend with you were all too fleeting." This admiration continues in his next letter (11 April 1907):

> I have the feeling of having made considerable inner progress since I got to know you personally; it seems to me that one can never quite understand your science unless one knows you in the flesh. Where so much still remains dark to us outsiders only faith can help; but the best and most effective faith is knowledge of your personality. Hence my visit to Vienna was a genuine confirmation.

Should one really assume that Jung as a young man deceived Freud persistently? Even more to the point, how should one judge this passage from a letter written six months later (28 October 1907): "I have a boundless admiration for you both as a man and a researcher. . . . [M]y veneration for you has something of the character of a 'religious' crush"? Such declarations sound spontaneous and were certainly not provoked by Freud. Did Jung also lie to Sabina Spielrein (1885–1941), the woman he loved passionately, when he wrote her (28 September 1908) after Freud's visit in Zurich the previous week:

> Prof. Freud spent an extended period at my house. During this time with him I had occasion, for the first time, really, to see this great man in my own world, detached from his milieu, and to understand him so much more profoundly than before. He is indeed an outstanding and decent human being, who, by virtue of his marvelous knowledge of human nature and his life experience, is able to see things far more comprehensively than I. Your notion on this point is correct. If earlier I only admired this man from afar, I now have actually grown very fond of him. As you will realize, I have used my time with Freud to good purpose. Many things have become clear to me. In short, it was good for me [Carotenuto, 1986, p. 194f.].[8]

This passage, too, is irreconcilable with an agonizing experience involving discovery of Freud's alleged intimate relationship with Minna Bernays.

Freud apparently was aware from the beginning of his relationship with Jung of the dangers that an all-too-acute transference harbors. He tried to reduce it

[8]The English version of Carotenuto (1982) does not contain the letters from Jung to Spielrein. The originals of these letters are in a later German edition (Carotenuto, 1986). Translations here by Marion Palmedo.

to a healthy level. Thus, when Jung confessed in his letter of 8 November 1907, "My old religiosity had secretly found in you a compensating factor which I had to come to terms with eventually," Freud replied (15 November 1907): "[A] transference on a religious basis would strike me as most disastrous; it could end only in apostasy. . . . I shall do my best to show you that I am unfit to be an object of worship." As we shall see, within a few years Freud succeeded, to a greater degree than he might have wished.

III

In his interview with Billinsky, Jung did not limit himself to his first visit in Vienna; he referred also to his trip with Freud to the United States, which covered the time from 20 August to 29 September 1909. At that juncture he got entangled in a contradiction that proves that Minna Bernays never confided in him. He told Billinsky (p. 42): ". . . [W]e [Freud and Jung] were together every day for some seven weeks. From the very beginning of our trip we started to analyze each other's dreams."[9] Is it probable that

---

[9]Groesbeck (1980) erroneously concludes from this remark that both had been in analysis with each other. But the passage, to be quoted (see p. 126), in which Jung taunts Freud for not having submitted to analysis whereas he had done so, makes it clear that only he had been analyzed. To analyze a friend's or acquaintance's dream was, in those years, a kind of parlor game. To give an example: Freud spoke positively of Johann Jakob Honegger (1885–1911), Jung's assistant, who "has made a splendid impression on me . . . by an attempt to analyse me" (2 February 1910), which can only have meant analysis by the interpretation of a dream. Jung had reported to Freud on 30 January 1910: "The man [Honegger] does excellent work, such as none of my pupils has produced before. He has also done a lot for me personally. I have had to hand over some of my dreams to him." It would be misleading to infer from that remark that Jung was in analysis with Honegger.

Freud analyzed Jung's dreams over a long period of time without noticing that Jung harbored an agonizing secret about his private life? Freud was more than a keen dream interpreter. He, like no one else, had the faculty of penetrating to the very bottom of a dream, which made him a kind of crystal gazer, as Mme. Choisy found out. After listening to a dream in her third analytic session, Freud maintained that she was of illegitimate birth. Having no trace of knowledge of it, she violently denied it, but the accuracy of Freud's interpretation was confirmed (Choisy, 1971). Thus, from one dream, after the shortest acquaintance, Freud divined the subject's most deeply repressed secret, a skeleton in the closet that the family—in vain, as it turned out—tried to keep from her. I have to ask again, is it probable, in view of such an uncanny faculty, that Freud was consistently deceived by Jung throughout their voyage? Even more to the point, there is one remark from which it appears that Jung considered himself to be in analysis with Freud, even if partly, by correspondence, a remark that implies he actually had been in regular treatment: "I am suffering all the agonies of a patient in analysis, riddling myself with every conceivable fear about the possible consequences of my confession" (2 November 1907).

Yet in his letter of 18 December 1912 he even boasted: "I am not in the least neurotic—touch wood! I have submitted *lege artis et tout humblement* to analysis and am much the better for it." Triumphantly he held his own allegedly successful analysis against Freud's self-analysis: "You know, of course, how far a patient gets with self-analysis: *not* out of neurosis—just like you" (Jung's emphasis). There is at least one error in Jung's boast: he was unaware that Freud would have insisted that his analysis of Jung was "incomplete," as Freud called analyses that had not been finished (1937, p. 219). That Jung's analysis was incomplete can be learned from his answer to the question (asked in an interview in 1959) of why as a preadolescent boy he was afraid of his mother at nighttime. When he replied, without hesitation, "I have not the slightest idea why" (McGuire and Hull, 1977, p. 427), he made clear his ignorance of the etiology of his childhood neurosis. Besides, his *Memories* abound in attestations that he was fully in the dark about his psychopathology. Thus, he was wrong when he thought that he had been successfully analyzed by Freud. But if he had been right, it would have amounted to an incident worthy of a science-fiction story, in which a person was successfully analyzed even though he kept to himself knowledge of his analyst's secret incestuous life.[10] This, of course, is an impossibility, and one wonders about Billinsky's naïveté in accepting Jung's report of dream analysis on the U.S. trip and his simultaneous insistence that "Freud had no idea that I knew about the triangle and his intimate relationship with his sister-in-law" (Billinsky, 1969, p. 42). One wonders on what grounds Jung could be so cocksure in 1909 that Minna Bernays had maintained the deception he attributed to her and had not broken down and confessed her indiscretion to Freud in order to free herself from the feeling of guilt that must necessarily have burdened her, if the interview recorded facts. After all, she had

---

[10]Gay (1988, p. 752f.), who used many of the same arguments (Eissler, 1982) in showing the falseness inherent in Jung's interview with Billinsky, disregarded this objection, although it carries the strongest weight.

to face her brother-in-law and alleged lover day by day.

IV

Another contradiction is puzzling. Assuming that Jung spoke to Billinsky in good faith, he would have had to be aware that he had admitted to having intentionally withheld associations to his dreams from Freud. Inescapably, recollections of Minna Bernays's communication would have crossed his mind while he was associating to his dreams at the time of the ocean crossing, not to mention during his analysis. Evidently he had no compunction about keeping them unverbalized, which makes it surprising to read, in the same passage of the interview:

> Freud had some dreams that bothered him very much. The dreams were about the triangle—Freud, his wife, and wife's younger sister. . . . [W]hen Freud told me about the dream in which his wife and her sister played important parts, I asked Freud to tell me some of his personal associations with the dream. He looked at me with bitterness and said, "I could tell you more, but I cannot risk my authority." That, of course, finished my attempt to deal with his dreams. . . . I could not accept Freud's placing authority above the truth [Billinsky, 1969, p. 42f.].

One may ask, in what way might Freud have placed authority above truth on that occasion? He was, if anything, as their correspondence proves, liberal in the transmission of personal details to Jung, but he would not have wanted the world, including

Jung, to know all his fantasies, forbidden impulses and the like. When admitting that in his associations he had reached the limit of what he was ready to reveal (an admission he made repeatedly when writing about his dreams), he was being honest. Jung, if his report to Billinsky should be correct, never told Freud when *he* had reached that limit. One searches in vain for a reason for his taking such vehement exception to Freud's refusal.

Jung referred to the same incident on at least three other occasions. In the letter in which he upheld himself as a paragon of mental health (3 December 1912) he reminded Freud of the reason that "our analysis . . . came to a stop." It was "your remark that you 'could not submit to analysis *without losing your authority.*' These words are engraved on my memory as a symbol of everything to come. I haven't eaten *my* words, however" (Jung's emphasis).

The second occasion is found in his *Memories, Dreams, Reflections* (Jung, 1961, p. 158). There he described what it was that

> proved to be a severe blow to the whole relationship. Freud had a dream—I would not think it right to air the problem it involved. I interpreted it as best I could, but added that a great deal more could be said about it if he would supply me with some additional details from his private life. Freud's response to these words was a curious look—a look of the utmost suspicion. Then he said, "But I cannot risk my authority!" At that moment he lost it altogether. That sentence burned itself into my memory; and in it the end of our relationship was already foreshadowed. Freud was placing personal authority above truth.

A third reference is found in the Notes of Jung's 1925 Seminar in Zurich (Jung, 1989, p. 22). It is essentially a slight variation of the previously cited accounts:

> We analyzed dreams each day, and it was then that I got an impression, a fatal one, of his limitations. . . . —I felt myself to be his son. Then something happened which put a stop to it. Freud had a dream on an important theme which I cannot mention. [I requested] some points about his private life. He looked at me with a peculiar expression of suspicion in his eyes and said: "I could tell you more but I can't risk my authority." Then I knew further analysis was impossible because he put authority above truth. I said I would have to stop there, and I never asked him again for material. You must understand that I talk here quite objectively, but I must include this experience with Freud, because it is the most important factor in my relation to him. He could not bear any criticism whatsoever.

Whoever believes that the last sentence (which is a total *non sequitur*) is more than an empty cliché only has to read Freud's letter of 15 June 1911, where he writes, "In matters of occultism I have grown humble. . . . I promise to believe anything that can be made to look reasonable. I shall not do so gladly, that you know. But my hubris has been shattered." Does this sound like a man who could not bear criticism?

In any event, Jung's claim that Freud's refusal "to risk authority" was "the most important factor" in his relation to Freud was to entangle him in a contradiction in his conversation with Billinsky. According to his Notes of 1925, when he spoke "quite objectively," his distrust in Freud started abruptly and was occasioned by a solitary remark of Freud's. According to the version he gave Billinsky, however, his relationship with Freud was disturbed from the beginning: "It was my knowledge of Freud's triangle that became a very important factor in my break with Freud" (Billinsky, 1969, p. 43). The two versions are different enough to arouse the suspicion that neither may have been correct.

Another oddity is connected with the episode. Two years after Jung had revealed the Minna Bernays story to Billinsky and had referred to the incestuous nature of Freud's dream, he was given the opportunity to comment on his knowledge of Freud in the aforementioned broadcast interview. He answered the interviewer's inquiry, ". . . what were the significant features of Freud's dreams that you noted?," with: "That is rather indiscreet to ask. . . . —there is such a thing as a professional secret." When the interviewer persisted, "He's been dead these many years," Jung replied, "Yes, but these regards last longer than life" (McGuire and Hull, 1977, p. 432). In his *Memories*, too, Jung said that he did not feel entitled to reveal the content of the dream in question (Jung, 1961, p. 158).[11]

One may ask whether Freud did in fact ever refer to "risking his authority" when he refused to divulge details of his private life. The answer is of less concern to one interested in Jung than it is to one interested in Freud. The statement sounds strange from his mouth, and if Jung had not brought it up in his letter

---

[11]Jung acted correctly when he upheld the professional obligation of discretion. Dr. Bennet's disbelief that Jung might have broken that obligation in speaking to Billinsky was all too well justified. Jung's violation of propriety is a further enigmatic aspect of that interview.

of 3 December 1912 without eliciting an objection from Freud, I, for one, would have doubted its authenticity, for hardly any stirrings toward authority on Freud's part can be discovered in their correspondence. Freud's silence on this topic in his reply to Jung could be taken as a confirmation of the remark's accuracy. Yet, one sometimes does not correct or refute a statement because to do so would require drawn-out explanations or lead to unending wrangles.

Be that as it may, one can only refer to Jung's letters, as was done on the occasion of the alleged agonizing contretemps during his first visit to Vienna. One should expect to find at least some traces of Jung's second great disappointment. Instead, Jung, who was not most prompt with his epistles, wrote immediately upon his return to Küsnacht (1 October 1909), "Here I stand on your doorstep with a letter of welcome to greet you in Vienna on resumption of work," adding, "I feel in top form and have become much more reasonable than you might suppose." This does not sound as if Freud had acted in an objectionable manner on their voyage. "On the journey back to Switzerland," Jung continued, "I never stopped analysing dreams and discovered some priceless jokes." This sounds as if Jung's dreams, rather than Freud's, had been at the center of their conversations. The next letter (14 October 1909) contains a truly surprising declaration: "Occasionally a spasm of homesickness for you comes over me, but only occasionally; otherwise I am back into my stride. The analysis on the voyage home has done me a lot of good." Has anyone written in such a spirit about a phase of his analysis during which he was allegedly severely traumatized by his analyst's conduct, as Jung averred later?

And Freud? He generally responded sensitively to disturbances in his relations to people close to him. He seemed to have been completely oblivious of what Jung alleges to have happened during the ocean crossing. His first letter after his return (4 October 1909) is touching in its tenderness: "Then a few addenda to the wonders of our trip. The day after we separated an incredible number of people looked amazingly like you; wherever I went in Hamburg, your light hat with the dark band kept turning up. And the same in Berlin. . . . My wife and children thank you kindly for your companionship during the trip, thanks to which I never felt that I was among strangers." To all appearances, their ties were stronger after their voyage than they had been before, and this may again weaken one's belief in Jung's later testimony.

V

On that dream-eventful crossing, Freud's dream was not the only one that would have consequences; there was another one, followed by even graver consequences, and this time it was one of Jung's. It was a long dream (Jung, 1961, p. 158f.) that should hold a place in the history of ideas, since it initiated Jung's introduction of the concept of the collective unconscious, which became the cornerstone of his analytical psychology. I have discussed this issue in detail in my 1982 publication. In the present context, the ending of the dream is pivotal.

The dream centered in a house with an upper story, a ground floor, a cellar and a deep cave. Each of the floors, according to Jung, represented a phase in the history of mankind, the cave being the most ancient. The ground was covered with "thick dust, . . . and in the dust were scattered bones and broken pottery, like remains of a primitive culture. I discovered two human skulls, obviously very old and half disintegrated. Then I awoke." When Jung told Freud the dream, he was mainly interested in the two skulls.

> He returned to them repeatedly, and urged me to find a *wish* in connection with them. What did I think about these skulls? And whose were they? I knew perfectly well, of course, what he was driving at: that secret death-wishes were concealed in the dream. "But what does he really expect of me?" I thought to myself. Toward whom would I have death-wishes? I felt violent resistance to any such interpretation. I also had some intimation of what the dream might really mean. But I did not then trust my own judgment, and wanted to hear Freud's opinion. I wanted to learn from him. Therefore I submitted to his intention and said, "My wife and my sister-in-law"—after all, I had to name someone whose death was worth the wishing! [Jung, 1961, p. 159f.; Jung's emphasis].

This can easily be demonstrated to be a string of rationalizations. Deceit was not warrantable by the necessity of testing Freud, because Jung knew, as he stated, what Freud's interpretation would be. He had analyzed a score of dreams in collaboration with Freud, had studied Freud's texts on dream interpretation. Even to his own ears, his explanation seemed to be incredible and therefore he had to add further rationalizations. He continued:

I would not have been able to present to Freud my own ideas on an interpretation of the dream without encountering incomprehension and vehement resistance. I did not feel up to quarreling with him, and I also feared that I might lose his friendship if I insisted on my own point of view. On the other hand, I wanted to know what he would make of my answer, and what his reaction would be if I deceived him by saying something that suited his theories. And so I told him a lie.

I was quite aware that my conduct was not above reproach, but *à la guerre, comme à la guerre!* It would have been impossible for me to afford him any insight into my mental world. The gulf between it and his was too great. In fact Freud seemed greatly relieved by my reply. I saw from this that he was completely helpless in dealing with certain kinds of dreams and had to take refuge in his doctrine. I realized that it was up to me to find out the real meaning of the dream [Jung, 1961, p. 160].

A comparison of Jung's *Memories* and the letters he wrote after his return to Europe makes the conclusion stringent that either one or the other contained a series of deceitful statements. Their discrepancy is extensive and goes far beyond the inaccuracy of detail that is unavoidable when events are recalled after decades. Furthermore, Jung's contemptuous remark about Freud being "helpless" vis-à-vis the interpretation of some dreams is all the more surprising in view of his report that, after his break with Freud, he went through a crisis in which he was at a complete loss regarding the interpretation of his own dreams, so much so that he came close to suicide (cf. p. 44).

So far as the dream of the two skulls is concerned, the key to it, according to Jung, was his preoccupation with the superiority of the historical School of Basel over Freud's naturalism. But as will be seen, Jung's mind was preoccupied with far less angelic problems during the ocean crossing. The true meaning of the dream becomes clear when another "lie," which he was most eager to conceal from the reader, comes to the fore. When he gave the reason for choosing wife and sister-in-law as presumptive associations to the two skulls—allegedly to test and please Freud—he added, "I was newly married at the time and knew perfectly well that there was nothing within myself which pointed to such wishes" (p. 44). Is it possible that Jung, when dictating his memoirs, forgot, by virtue of his 80-some years, his passionate love affair with Sabina Spielrein, under the impact of which he still was smarting during the months of his U.S. trip? Perhaps he did not anticipate that his intimate letters would ever be published. In one of them, that of 4 December 1908, which Spielrein made known to Freud in her letter of 13 June 1909, one finds comments on his marriage to which greater authenticity must be attributed than to those one finds in his *Memories*.

> When love for a woman awakens within me, the first thing I feel is regret, pity for the poor woman who dreams of eternal faithfulness and other impossibilities and is slated for a rude awakening. Therefore, if one is already married, it is better to engage in this lie only once and do penance for it immediately than to repeat the experiment again and again, lying again and again, disappointing someone [Carotenuto, 1982, p. 102].

How did Jung's love affair with Sabina Spielrein come about? Her parents had brought her to Zurich in 1904 for treatment of a serious nervous disorder. She was treated by Jung for a psychotic spell of hysteria as an inpatient at the Burghölzli Clinic for ten months, and later as an outpatient. She recovered to the extent that she was able to study medicine and graduate in 1909.[12] In order to give an approximate impression of her and Jung's relationship, I shall let her speak.

In her diary, which covers the years from 1909 to 1912, she wrote: "He [Jung] admitted to me that so far he knew no female who could replace me. It was as if he had a necklace in which all his other admirers were—pearls, and I—the medallion" (Carotenuto, 1982, p. 8). In a letter to Freud she stated, "He [Jung] preached polygamy; his wife was supposed to have no objection, etc., etc." (p. 93). And yet, in his memoirs Jung claims that his marriage was undisturbed (Jung, 1961, p. 160).

When rumors of their relationship reached Vienna, Jung was ready to deny everything. "The story [the rumor that had reached Freud]," he wrote (11 March 1909), ". . . is Chinese to me. I've never really had a mistress and am the most innocent of spouses. Hence my terrific moral reaction! I simply cannot imagine who it might have been. I don't think it is the same lady. Such stories give me the horrors."

He evidently tried initially to deceive Freud, just as he later did the reader of his memoirs. But success was denied to his attempt at deceiving Freud, and

---

[12]In 1912 she married in Zurich and had two daughters. She became a psychoanalyst and was a member of the group in Vienna. In 1923 she returned to her native Russia. She and her two daughters were executed by the Germans in 1941. She published 33 papers, some of lasting importance; in one of them she anticipated Freud's theory of the death drive.

he finally acknowledged (21 June 1909) that he had committed "a piece of knavery." This throws an unexpected light on Jung's narrative in the memoirs (1961, p. 159f.). It stands to reason that Jung, being partially dependent on his wife's wealth but not finding contentment and happiness in marriage, and having to fear lest his former patient might cause scandal, divorce and loss of standing in the community, harbored aggressive feelings against both wife and lover. Freud, who was fully informed of the affair at the time of the ocean crossing, cannot have doubted the meaning of the two skulls. It is improbable that he urged Jung to associate to the dream element at all, since evidently they must have discussed at great length the nerve-racking problem Jung had to face with his lover. The two remarks quoted above—"I feel in top form and have become much more reasonable than you might suppose" (1 October 1909), and, "The analysis on the voyage home has done me a lot of good" (14 October 1909)—bear witness to the vast relief that his discussions with Freud had granted him after he had gone through a most perilous reality situation.

It is difficult to evade the impression that the old man, when dictating his memoirs, was still haunted by the many humiliating experiences of 1909. If we envision a cross section through Jung's troubled mind at the time of the ocean voyages, it becomes apparent why he found it necessary to make the reader believe that his chief preoccupation was with the historical School of Basel. Jung, if anyone, was a proud and self-righteous man. The year 1909, when he had to run the gauntlet, must have left a gangrenous spot in his memory and self-esteem. Some passages from the

Freud-Jung correspondence will illustrate this. Jung to Freud (4 June 1909):

> Spielrein is the person I wrote you about. She was published in abbreviated form in my Amsterdam lecture of blessed memory. She was, so to speak, my test case, for which reason I remembered her with special gratitude and affection. Since I knew from experience that she would immediately relapse if I withdrew my support, I prolonged the relationship over the years and in the end found myself morally obliged, as it were, to devote a large measure of friendship to her, until I saw that an unintended wheel had started turning, whereupon I finally broke with her. She was, of course, systematically planning my seduction, which I considered inopportune. Now she is seeking revenge. Lately she has been spreading a rumor that I shall soon get a divorce from my wife and marry a certain girl student, which has thrown not a few of my colleagues into a flutter. What she is now planning is unknown to me. Nothing good, I suspect, unless perhaps you are imposed upon to act as a go-between. I need hardly say that I have made a clean break.

In his letter of 7 June 1909 Freud told Jung he would see Spielrein, and continued:

> Such experiences, though painful, are necessary and hard to avoid. Without them we cannot really know life and what we are dealing with. I myself have never been taken in quite so badly, but I have come very close to it a number of times and had a narrow escape. I believe that only grim necessities weighing on my work, and the fact that I was ten years older than yourself when I came to psychoanalysis, have saved

me from similar experiences. But no lasting harm is done. They help us to develop the thick skin we need and to dominate "countertransference," which is after all a permanent problem for us; they teach us to displace our own affects to best advantage. They are a "blessing in disguise."

In response, Jung (12 June 1909) made a concession to Freud that may have left an unpleasant taste in his mouth:

I had to tell myself that if a friend or colleague of mine had been in the same difficult situation I would have written in the same vein [as Freud did in his answer]. I had to tell myself this because my father complex kept on insinuating that you would not take it as you did but would give me a dressing-down more or less disguised in the mantle of brotherly love. For actually it is too stupid that I of all people, your "son and heir," should squander your heritage so heedlessly, as though I had known nothing of all these things.

In his next letter (21 June 1909) Jung again expressed his feeling of remorse:

I . . . deplore the sins I have committed, for I am largely to blame for the high-flying hopes of my former patient. So, in accordance with my original principle of taking everyone seriously to the uttermost limit, I discussed with her [Spielrein] the problem of the child [i.e., having a child with her], imagining that I was talking theoretically, but naturally Eros was lurking in the background. Thus I imputed all the other wishes and hopes entirely to my patient without seeing the same thing in myself. When the situation had become so tense that the continued perseveration of the relationship could be rounded out only by sexual acts, I defended myself in a manner that cannot be justified morally. Caught in my delusion that I was the victim of the sexual wiles of my patient, I wrote to her mother that I was not the gratifier of her daughter's sexual desires but merely her doctor, and that she should free me from her. In view of the fact that the patient had shortly before been my friend and enjoyed my full confidence, my action was a piece of knavery which I very reluctantly confess to you as my father. . . . I ask your pardon many times, for it was my stupidity that drew you into this imbroglio.

Indeed, most of Jung's utterances sound strange coming from a man who allegedly knew all along, through Minna Bernays's indiscretion, that his mentor's offense against standards of conduct was worse than his own.

Freud replied (30 June 1909):

[Your letter] would have reconciled me to greater misdeeds on your part; perhaps I am already too biased in your favor. Immediately after receiving your letter I wrote Fräulein Sp. a few amiable lines, giving her satisfaction, and today received an answer from her. . . . Don't find fault with yourself for drawing me into it; it was not your doing but hers. And the matter has ended in a manner satisfactory to all.

And Jung responded on 10 July 1909: ". . . I want to thank you very much for your kind help in the Spielrein matter, which has now settled itself so satisfactorily. Once again I took too black a view."

Freud acted with utmost tact and gentleness, for which Jung perhaps never forgave him and thus had to make him appear as a person with a rigid, limited mind. Posterity, too, had little understanding and took a critical attitude toward Freud for having given Jung his full support (e.g., Cremerius in his Foreword to Carotenuto, 1986).

It looks as if in his *Memories* and in talking to Billinsky, Jung tried to undo the humiliation of 1909 by boldly converting it into its opposite. In those reports, under the influence of memories of distressing events, Jung confabulated about his analyst's sex life and about events that transpired during the ocean crossing; in the latter connection he portrayed himself as successful in dissembling associations to his own dream and in concealing awareness of his analyst's alleged sexual misconduct. It is breathtaking to watch Jung stepping into a hornet's nest of misstatements, inventions, and outright lies told in order to settle an old grudge dating back to a time when he lost face as a panicky, guilty-ridden sinner. The resulting story cannot possibly have taken place as stated and lays Jung open as a man who does not flinch from denigrating Freud when it serves to increment his own stature.

But to return to the dream of the multi-storied house above the deep cave, its greater importance goes beyond the biographical implications. It was, in Jung's words, the inception of his theory of the collective unconscious. As demonstrated above, the dream was a personal one and becomes understandable as a derivative of the rage and vindictiveness he felt toward wife and lover. In Jung's view, however, the two skulls were elevated to the status of remnants of prehistoric creatures, for he identified them as belonging to *Homo neanderthalensis* and *Pithecanthropus*. He promulgated them as his "real associations to the dream" (Jung, 1976, p. 214) and escaped the impact of his own guilt by shifting personal biography to primeval ancestors. One feels tempted to extend to his subsequent theory of the collective unconscious the same escapist function that is discovered in Jung's response to the dream that prompted his theory. Both served as a glittering facade covering a distressing personal (biographical) truth. The denial of the true nature of the unconscious secured Jung fame all over the world.

Jung's use of the dream in the *Memories* to diminish Freud by making him appear a biased, narrow mind that could be easily fooled was an act of ingratitude and petty revenge. Jung complained to Freud (7 May 1908) that Karl Abraham (1877–1925), his colleague, "is simply not a gentleman. . . . just about the worst thing that can happen to anyone." The "worst thing" perceived in others is sometimes a projection, as in Jung's case. Not only was the way he treated Freud far from gentlemanly behavior, but there were also other incidents that suggest Jung's deficiency in fairness. I shall limit myself to two of them.

An otherwise unpublished letter written by Jung to M. Kranefeldt, a former pupil of his, who was a Board member of the Berlin Institute of Psychotherapy after the takeover in 1933 by the National Socialists, contains this passage:

> As is known, one cannot do anything against stupidity, but in this instance the Aryan people can point out that with Freud and Adler, specific Jewish points of view are publicly preached and, as can be proved likewise, points of view that have an essentially erosive character. If the proclamation of this Jewish gospel is agreeable to the government, then so be it.

> Otherwise, there is also the possibility that this would not be agreeable to the government . . . [Stargardt, n.d.; Ostow, 1977].

This was written in 1934 and aimed at helping to bring about the government's suppression of a psychological school that at that time enjoyed greater public repute than his own.

The other example shows up in a letter to Sabina Spielrein's mother when she became alarmed by the possibility that her daughter might have an affair with Jung. She implored him not to "corrupt" her, now that he had healed her, he replied that he did not have the obligation of a physician because he never requested a fee. If she wanted him to stay within the limits imposed upon the medical profession, she should send him a fee to recompense him for his professional services. To close his letter, he wrote, "My fee is 10 francs per consultation. I advise you to choose the prosaic solution, since that is the more prudent one and creates no obligations for the future. With friendly good wishes, etc." (Carotenuto, 1982, p. 94). As a matter of fact, a letter to Sabina (12 August 1908) ends with, "Thank you very much for the money, which I received promptly" (Carotenuto, 1986, p. 193).

VI

In order to come closer to an understanding of the Billinsky interview, one has to take cognizance of the psychosis that followed Jung's break with Freud—or probably had started shortly before—as well as his serious childhood psychopathology. Both topics would deserve detailed presentation, but only a shortened version is feasible in this context. Jung's *Memories, Dreams, Reflections* (Jung, 1961) should not be neglected, for in it both subjects appear with surprising clarity.

The break itself took a rapid course. At the beginning of the year 1912, Jung sent Freud his greetings for the New Year—written at a time when the year had already started, a delay that was not exceptional for him. The letter's second sentence was: "May the new year add many a leaf to the laurel crown of your undying fame and open new fields for our movement" (2 January 1912). No one would have guessed from that reverential introduction that it would be a year of vehement attacks against Freud that ultimately enforced a final break.

Persons of exceptional talent engaged in passionate struggles with ideas and driven toward original creations sometimes feel compelled to bid a stormy farewell to their teachers. Freud, who hardly had had the opportunity to go through a manifest, strong Oedipus conflict—for his father was most generous and kind to him and had all the characteristics of a benevolent grandfather—turned against Breuer, to whom he owed an inordinate debt, as a substitute, and broke with him aggressively with such finality that he never again exposed himself to his sight although they lived in the same city. But the years of falling-out were accompanied by intensive creativity, leading to the writing of *The Interpretation of Dreams* (1900). Historians biased in favor of Wilhelm Fliess may say Freud rebelled ungratefully against Fliess—which he did not do. But even if he had done so, it would have been in a phase that led to the "Three Essays on the Theory of Sexuality" (1905), another creative peak. But what about Jung? He reports, in his *Memories* (Jung, 1961, p. 193): "After the completion of *The Psychology of the Unconscious* I found myself utterly incapable of reading a scientific book. This went on for three years. I felt I could no longer keep up with the world of the intellect, nor would I have been able to talk about what really preoccupied me." Why should a scholar who asked to be credited with new discoveries, the revision of existing insights, as he told Freud, suddenly fall into complete emptiness after he succeeded in freeing himself of what he had called oppressive authority? This is all the more surprising since he felt he had become the trumpeter of a liberated generation. In his letter of 15 November 1912, he had hurled these words at Freud:

> I shall continue to go my own way undaunted. . . . I propose to let tolerance prevail in the *Jahrbuch* [whose editor he was] so that everyone can develop in his own way. Only when granted freedom do people give of their best. We should not forget that the history of human truths is also the history of human errors. So let us give the well-meant error its rightful place.

In a perusal of Jung's *Memories*, one encounters a sequence of four phases following his break with Freud that carry the stigmata of the course of a psychosis.

(1) Phase of the tabula rasa: "After the parting of the ways with Freud, a period of inner uncertainty began for me. It would be no exaggeration to call it a

state of disorientation. I felt totally suspended in mid-air, for I had not yet found my own footing." These are the sentences with which Jung introduces the chapter "Confrontation with the Unconscious" (Jung, 1961, p. 170) (which, after years of psychiatric and psychoanalytic clinical practice, it would have been more appropriate to call "Confrontation with *My* Unconscious"). Jung tried to eschew awareness of any earlier psychiatric experiences and to listen to his patients without bringing "any theoretical premises to bear upon them" (p. 170). Yet, "the need for a criterion grew more and more pressing" (p. 171).

In the past he thought that he had found the key to mythology and was free "to unlock all the gates of the unconscious psyche" (p. 171). This led him to ask, ". . . what is . . . the myth in which you do live?" (p. 171). At this point he "stopped thinking. I had reached a dead end" (p. 171), for he was unable to define his own myth. This statement indeed contradicts almost every accusation he had lodged against Freud a short time before. He had boasted to Freud that he was well analyzed and yet he found himself in a state of disorientation. He had left Freud allegedly because Freud took a critical attitude toward his discovery, but he himself felt he had to start all over again, evidently not trusting the solidity of his own theory. The phase under discussion proves that it was not Freud's acting out or other inappropriate responses that drove him away but an inner conflict he tried in vain to escape by taking flight from Freud. The next phase confirms this.

(2) Phase of regression: Around Christmas of 1912 Jung had a long dream that he was unable to interpret. It is noteworthy that he acted as if he had never

before interpreted his own or Freud's or his patients' dreams by gathering free associations. What came to his mind were, with one exception, sophisticated historical details which, unlike free associations, did not reveal his inner life. But among the historical images there was ". . . a little girl, about eight years of age, with golden blond hair. . . . [who] tenderly placed her arms around my neck. Then she suddenly vanished" (p. 171f.). It did not strike him that his daughter Agäthli was eight years old at that time. In this example, too, it is easy to see why dream interpretation in terms of the collective unconscious, with its historical foundation, is more comfortable than in personal, biographical terms.

Frightening fantasies arose, of corpses in crematory ovens that were discovered to be still alive, dreams about mummified corpses that he could revive by looking at them. The inner pressure became so strong "that I suspected there was some psychic disturbance in myself" (p. 173). He thought something in his past might have brought on that state, but he had to admit ignorance. "Thereupon I said to myself, 'Since I know nothing at all, I shall simply do whatever occurs to me' " (p. 173). A spell of intense repetition of childhood games set in, in which he was concerned with building cottages and castles on the lake shore, collecting pebbles, and the like. It is most extraordinary that a 37-year-old father should indulge for a long time in childhood play alone at the shore, without permitting or inviting the company of his five-year-old son. It probably denotes the extreme degree of isolation into which he had plunged. I would suggest, tentatively, that the desire for independence that had made him leave Freud, but which he was unable to maintain, precipitated a regression to infantile narcissistic independence and omnipotence. It was he who was able to give life to corpses; his father, a clergyman, could only bury them.

(3) Phase of the doomed world: In the fall of 1913 the world started to change its appearance:

> The atmosphere actually seemed to me darker than it had been. It was as though the sense of oppression no longer sprang exclusively from a psychic situation, but from concrete reality. This feeling grew more and more intense.
>
> In October, while I was alone on a journey, I was suddenly seized by an overpowering vision: I saw a monstrous flood covering all the northern and low-lying lands between the North Sea and the Alps. When it came up to Switzerland I saw that the mountains grew higher and higher to protect our country. I realized that a frightful catastrophe was in progress. I saw the mighty yellow waves, the floating rubble of civilization, and the drowned bodies of uncounted thousands. Then the whole sea turned to blood. This vision lasted about one hour. I was perplexed and nauseated, and ashamed of my weakness [p. 175].

When the same vision recurred, he decided that he "was menaced by a psychosis" (p. 176).

In his dreams, the end-of-the-world vision was then repeated in a different shape, and he started to write down his fantasies. He stood helpless before an alien world, feeling as if gigantic blocks of stone were tumbling down on him. Others, like Hölderlin and Nietzsche, he mused, were shattered by such assaults, "[b]ut there was a demonic strength in me" (p. 177).

To the extent that I managed to translate the emotions into images—that is to say, to find the images which were concealed in the emotions—I was inwardly calmed. . . . Had I left those images hidden in the emotions, I might have been torn to pieces by them. There is a chance that I might have succeeded in splitting them off; but in that case I would inexorably have fallen into a neurosis and so been ultimately destroyed by them anyhow. As a result of my experiment I learned how helpful it can be, from the therapeutic point of view, to find the particular images which lie behind emotions [p. 177].

Did Jung have to make that experiment to find the truth he propounds here? One might ask what he had been doing during the preceding half decade in his clinical practice under Freud's guidance if not rendering explicit images that were concealed in emotions. Evidently he was unaware that his summary outline of what made his survival possible echoed precisely what he had learned from Freud.

Yet an almost unconquerable resistance prevented him from putting his fantasies on paper. On December 12, 1913, he made a final resolution: "I was . . . thinking over my fears. Then I let myself drop. Suddenly it was as though the ground literally gave way beneath my feet, and I plunged down into dark depths" (p. 179).

In deep regression, a mental process may be transmuted into a physical form; a prerequisite is a loosening of the body image. "Sometimes," he continued, "it was as if I were hearing it [what he was writing down] with my ears, sometimes feeling it with my mouth, as if my tongue were formulating words; now and then I heard myself whispering aloud" (p. 178).

The body scheme became unsettled. This gruesome phase culminated in a long dream in which he killed Siegfried and which brought him close to suicide. A voice within said: " 'You *must* understand the dream, and must do so at once! . . . If you do not understand the dream, you must shoot yourself!' " (p. 180; Jung's emphasis). He had a loaded revolver in his night table. It did not take long until the solution came to his mind:

> Siegfried, I thought, represents what the Germans want to achieve, heroically to impose their will, have their own way. "Where there is a will there is a way!" I had wanted to do the same. But now that was no longer possible. The dream showed that the attitude embodied by Siegfried, the hero, no longer suited me. Therefore it had to be killed.
>
> After the deed I felt an overpowering compassion, as though I myself had been shot: a sign of my secret identity with Siegfried, as well as of the grief a man feels when he is forced to sacrifice his ideal and his conscious attitudes [p. 180].

Here again one notices the consolation provided by the flight into the collective unconscious. A conflict about a philosophical conviction, about the necessity of having to change one's philosophical stance, could never have the power of producing a dream in which an emotional upheaval threatens the dreamer's life: "Filled with disgust and remorse for having destroyed something so great and beautiful, I turned to flee, impelled by the fear that the murder might be discovered. But a tremendous downfall of rain began, and I knew that it would wipe out all traces of the deed. I had escaped the danger of discovery; life could go on, but an unbearable feeling of guilt re-mained" (p. 180).

Even when all traces are wiped out, some hands, as Lady Macbeth had to find out, "will ne'er be clean," even after a tremendous downfall of rain. An unbearable feeling of guilt may remain when the crime is child murder—which is as much at the center of Lady Macbeth's nightmares as it is at the center of the dream that endangered Jung's life, when it peremptorily demanded to be interpreted. Some of the dream elements and associations strongly support that interpretation: the central figure, Siegfried, who is the epitome of a son; the dreamer's secret identity with Siegfried; the overpowering compassion; the sacrifice of an ideal.

There is biographical material that confirms the fact of Jung's ambivalence toward his son. The shattering dream was dreamt during the Advent season of 1913, and his son had been born the day before the first Advent Sunday, on November 28, 1908. His response to the newborn had been one of ambivalence from the beginning. He felt threatened by him, as his an-swer to Freud's congratulatory telegram shows: "Too bad," he wrote, "we aren't peasants any more, other-wise I could say: Now that I have a son I can depart in peace. A great deal more could be said on this complex-theme" (3 December 1908). Later, in con-junction with a mythological discussion, he wrote Freud, "The advent of the next generation is the be-ginning of the end" (26 June 1910). And in *Psychology of the Unconscious*, he expressed the threat even more explicitly:

> To be fruitful means, indeed, to destroy one's self, because with the rise of the succeeding generation

the previous one has passed beyond its highest point; thus our descendants are our most dangerous enemies, whom we cannot overcome, for they will outlive us, and, therefore, without fail, will take the power from our enfeebled hands [Jung, 1916, p. 117].

The unconscious death wish against his only son, who became five years old at the time of the dream (which coincided with the sixth month of his wife's fifth pregnancy), was a forceful impulse, for the son was at the peak of his oedipal stirrings, on the verge of entering the latency period. That time, when a child's prospective adulthood becomes visible, even if only in a vague outline, is critical not only for the child but frequently also for the father.

The third phase can be summarized as one in which Jung, after having eliminated Freud, the father, having slain the son and having destroyed the world by withdrawal, had reached the greatest possible depth of aloneness. Now his mind had arrived at the point where it was forced outward again.

(4) Phase of restitution and aggrandizement: From this solitude as a starting point, the mind, as Freud described in his paper on narcissism (1914), builds up a new world on its own terms. The new world shows the earmark of its creator, who has risen phoenix-like from the ashes.

This sequence of events is confirmed by Jung's description of a fantasy of his setting out on a journey involving a deep descent until "I found myself at the edge of a cosmic abyss. . . . I had the feeling that I was in the land of the dead" (Jung, 1961, p. 181). There he met the personages who would lead him back into a balanced existence. He caught sight of an old man and a beautiful girl, Elijah and Salome. "Elijah and I had a long conversation which, however, I did not understand" (1961, p. 181). He associated the Biblical figures with his father, who was a clergyman. The Elijah figure, which might have reminded him also of Freud, eventually grew into the figure Philemon, who "was a pagan and brought with him an Egypto-Hellenistic atmosphere with a Gnostic coloration" (p. 182). Evidently Philemon was distant enough from Freud and the clergyman father to be acceptable as a new guru. Philemon taught him "that there are things in the psyche which [one does] not produce, but which produce themselves and have their own life. . . . Psychologically, Philemon represented superior insight. He was a mysterious figure to me. At times he seemed to me quite real, as if he were a living personality. I went walking up and down the garden with him, and to me he was what the Indians call a guru" (p. 183).

Oddly enough, with the appearance of new, superior personifications Jung did not feel enriched but personally defeated, because to him it signified proof of his ignorance, and he feared an endless succession of figures who might affect him in the same way. But he was protected by "Philemon, whom in this respect I had willy-nilly to recognize as my psychagogue" (p. 184). It is noteworthy that Jung never acknowledged Philemon's subjective origin. "More than 15 years later" he was to learn from an Indian whose guru had died centuries ago that "[m]ost people have living gurus. But there are always some people who have a spirit for a teacher" (p. 183), and Jung was reminded of Philemon: apparently Jung, too, had the extraordinary privilege of being guided by a spirit dead for centuries. Consequently he recognized that an experiment had been conducted on him at that time in which he lost the autonomy of intellectual processes.

At any rate, in Philemon he found a substitute for Freud. He found a new father, who had descended from times immemorial to impart primordial wisdom to him. Philemon was not a competitor. Only Jung knew him, and with him he could maintain a conflict-free relationship. He was now able to announce to the world a new dogma whose true founder remained anonymous. Thus the deep wound that he had suffered by wresting himself away from Freud was superficially healed, and yet it festered enough to force him to say derogatory words about his first guru.

The empirically oriented psychologist will hardly follow Jung in his explanation of Philemon. He will judge Philemon's teachings as a derivative of Jung's own ideation and philosophy. One can study here with particular clarity Freud's theory, mentioned above, that after regression the subject finds his way back toward a new reality that is partly derived from the subject's personal world. This also happened with Philemon, who taught his disciple that there are things in the psyche that "produce themselves and have their own life," which is nothing more or less than the collective unconscious. Such a process more frequently than not leads to self-aggrandizement, which, in Jung's case, came to the fore even before the process came to rest. It was a peak experience in the strange world of those years and occurred in 1916:

Around five o'clock in the afternoon on Sunday the front doorbell began ringing frantically. It was a bright summer day; the two maids were in the kitchen, from which the open square outside the front door could be seen. Everyone immediately looked to see who was there, but there was no one in sight. I was sitting near the doorbell, and not only heard it but saw it moving. We all simply stared at one another. The atmosphere was thick, believe me! Then I knew that something had to happen. The whole house was filled as if there were a crowd present, crammed full of spirits. They were packed deep right up to the door, and the air was so thick it was scarcely possible to breathe. As for myself, I was all a-quiver with the question: "For God's sake, what in the world is this?" Then they cried out in chorus, "We have come back from Jerusalem where we found not what we sought." That is the beginning of the *Septem Sermones* [1961, p. 190f.].

The spirits, in other words, not having found what they sought in Jerusalem, the city where Christ had lived, preached and died, had come to Küsnacht and found it there. Evidently a new Gospel, superseding its four predecessors, had to be created. The *Septem Sermones ad Mortuos* were created under a grave inner onslaught. The beginning is characteristic of their emptiness: "Harken: I begin with nothingness. Nothingness is the same as fullness" (Jung, 1961, p. 379). Jung gave loose rein to meaningless paradoxes. "Later," we learn from Aniela Jaffé, who recorded and edited the *Memories*, "he [Jung] described it as a sin of his youth and regretted it" (p. 378). But Jung was over 40 years old when he wrote the *Septem Sermones*. To be sure, works created in phases of creative illness are often repudiated later by their author because of their all-too radical originality; however, although the editor informs us that one finds in the

Sermons "anticipations of ideas that were to figure later in his [Jung's] scientific writings, more specifically concerning the polaristic nature of the psyche, of life in general, and of all psychological statements" (p. 378), no ghost come from the grave is necessary to tell us this. Therefore, I doubt that the *Septem Sermones* are the product of a creative illness, as Ellenberger (1970, p. 672) suggests.[13]

There are other signs of grandiosity to be found in his *Memories*. He liked to entertain the idea that he might be a descendant of Goethe—which he was not (1961, pp. 35–36, n. 1; p. 234). Freud went along with the myth, with a twinkle in his eye (as, for instance, in his letter of 22 January 1911). As noted above, Jung felt he was stronger in enduring the onslaughts of fantasies than were "Nietzsche and Hölderlin, and many others" (p. 177); he thought himself to be in the possession of faculties denied to others (p. 355). One finds pronouncements like these: "[T]he pattern of my relationship to the world was already prefigured: today as then [in youth] I am solitary, because I know things and must hint at things which other people do not know, and usually do not even want to know" (p. 41f.). Or, "I do not know what started me off perceiving the stream of life" (p. 356). More could be cited. Evidently he believed that he had at his command visionary and intuitive powers that made him incomparable to others; in the last chapter of his *Memories* he indulges in long passages that show him as his own *laudator maximus*.

I have presented only a few highlights of the personal turmoil inherent in the four phases that filled

---

[13]Jung seems to have held the Sermons in high esteem. They were privately printed. Occasionally he gave a copy to a friend as a gift (Jung, 1961, p. 378).

the years after Jung's separation from Freud. One asks, how did he manage throughout all that time to maintain the appearance of a well organized, undisturbed, middle-class citizen? He gives the following explanation:

> My family and my profession remained the base to which I could always return, assuring me that I was an actually existing, ordinary person. The unconscious contents could have driven me out of my wits. But my family, and the knowledge: I have a medical diploma from a Swiss university, I must help my patients, I have a wife and five children, I live at 228 Seestrasse In Küsnacht—these were actualities which made demands upon me and proved to me again and again that I really existed [1961, p. 189].

Some may dispute the diagnostic conclusion I have drawn from the evidence at hand, but when someone has to memorize the data of his daily existence in order to preserve his sanity, he is going through a process that has not left the foundation of his personality unscathed. The exploration of Jung's childhood is expedient at this point.

VII

In my estimation it was of pivotal importance that Jung had an older brother, born 23 months earlier than he (Ellenberger, 1970, p. 662), who had died a few days after birth. The death of an older sibling prior to a child's own birth is often found to have been the seed of later severe psychopathology. The parents, when looking lovingly at the child, are thinking of his vanished predecessor. This casts a shadow on the existence of the survivor, who never becomes aware of the ghost that stands between him and his parents. Rivalry with the invisible must create confusion in the child. When Jung reports having had, in his early childhood, an "unconscious suicidal urge . . . a fatal resistance to life in this world" (Jung, 1961, p. 9) without further comment, and when he speaks of his belief in ghosts and the great role that they and spirits played in his life, all this suggests symptoms that followed from conflicts about the dead brother. Given that ghosts nowadays live predominantly in Switzerland (if not England, too), Jung's belief in ghosts may not be as idiosyncratic as it appears. Nevertheless, his early preoccupation with corpses and funerals may have been connected with the dead brother.

If the parents had been consciously or unconsciously preoccupied with their first-born when attending to the second son, the infant would rarely have received the feeling of their full presence, which would have determined a reduction in his own feeling of a full existence in this world. Even though I may overrate the importance of the dead brother, its echo is heard in a severe disturbance of ego, or self-feeling. Between the ages of seven and nine Jung felt compelled to sit on a special stone—his stone—and ruminate for hours as to whether he was the one who was sitting on the stone, or whether he was the stone on which he was sitting. His doubts went so far that he would become confused and had to brood about "who was what now" (p. 20). This may have been the foundation of an ego-disturbance that appeared not much later: he was "actually two different persons . . . the schoolboy who could not grasp algebra," as well as an important man, "a high authority . . . an old man who lived in the eighteenth century" (1961, p. 33f.). "These . . . impressions . . . coalesced into a coherent picture: of myself living in two ages simultaneously, and being two different persons" (p. 35).[14] He thereupon developed personality No. 1, which was turned toward external reality, and personality No. 2, which was kept as his deepest secret.

He denied that this division was in any way connected "with a 'split' or dissociation in the ordinary medical sense" (p. 45). Indeed, one observes strange, sometimes even bizarre features in talented personalities, not to mention geniuses. There are no set rules on how to distinguish disease and creative process, although they are totally different in structure, despite superficial and sometimes even extensive similarity. Yet in Jung's instance, the megalomania-like outcome speaks in favor of the basically pathological nature of the split. "Besides his world [personality No. 1, incorporating the schoolboy, vanity and meanness]," he wrote,

> there existed another realm, like a temple in which anyone who entered was transformed and suddenly overpowered by a vision of the whole cosmos, so that he could only marvel and admire, forgetful of himself. Here lived the "Other," who knew God as a hidden, personal, and at the same time suprapersonal

[14]Possibly this was a preliminary step on the way toward the formation of Philemon.

secret. Here nothing separated man from God; indeed, it was as though the human mind looked down upon Creation simultaneously with God [1961, p. 45].

A part of his personality was confluent with God. "At such times," he wrote, "I *knew* I was worthy of myself, that I was my true self. As soon as I was alone, I could pass over into this state. I therefore sought the peace and solitude of the 'Other,' personality No. 2" (p. 45; Jung's emphasis). Evidently the true self was God-like, a view that demonstrates the youngster's self-aggrandizement.

Personality No. 2 can possibly be traced to a fetish Jung constructed at age ten. "My disunion with myself and uncertainty in the world at large" (p. 21) led him to carve a little manikin into the end of a wooden ruler, which he hid away in the attic and visited with some regularity to perform a kind of solemn ritual. That most interesting creature initially absorbed all the secrets that would later form personality No. 2.

I must forgo a discussion of the rich psychopathology of Jung's early years, except for a blasphemous idea, which almost defeated him, and the most astounding method by which the boy laid it to rest. The sinful, obsessive thought, against which he fought a long time and which he finally could no longer hold back, but had to "let . . . come," was this. "I saw before me the cathedral, the blue sky. God sits on His golden throne, high above the world—and from under the throne an enormous turd falls upon the sparkling new roof, shatters it, and breaks the walls of the cathedral asunder" (p. 39). The child was thrown into a devastating conflict by his blasphemy and feared eternal damnation. Only by using a convoluted chain of syllogisms did he finally reach redemption and salvation. The solution was brought about by the conviction that God was testing him, and that by sinning he manifested his obedience toward God. It is indeed worthwhile to listen to some of his syllogisms.

"Who makes me think that God destroys His Church in this abominable manner? . . . I felt absolutely sure that it was not myself who had invented these thoughts and images" (p. 47). If God, despite His almightiness, did not free him from the obsession to sin, then He wanted to test the boy's obedience: "Is it possible that God wishes to see whether I am capable of obeying His will even though my faith and my reason raise before me the specters of death and hell?" (p. 39). Thus the child reached the point of being able to sin without feelings of guilt. He accomplished the extraordinary feat of transforming his aggression against the Holy Spirit, the greatest sin, into an act of "obedience which brought me grace" and which let him experience "what God's grace was. One must be utterly abandoned to God; nothing matters but fulfilling His will" (p. 40)[15] He thus achieved as a child what man rarely achieves—he had become immune to the feeling of guilt and the inner need to be punished, the two companions of sinners. This was an attainment fraught with dangers, since a child who drops all restraints and achieves tranquility of mind by uttering blasphemy, actions which are taken in order to draw closer to God's throne, lays the foundation of a serious character defect. For not only had

[15]The child's way of reasoning is reminiscent of Alan of Lille's (d. 1203) saying, "When the compulsion is greater the sin is slighter."

he laid to rest all potential self-reproaches but, perhaps even more dangerous, by dint of his reasoning he convinced himself that blasphemy was what his father, who was following the Bible and stayed away from sin, "had not understood; . . . he had failed to experience the will of God" (p. 40). Thus, he attained prematurely and in a pathological way superiority over his father. Understandably, this victory represented to him a notable achievement.

Jung speaks off and on of the secret of being in direct contact with God by sinning, and therefore being superior, not only to his father, but to others as well. To understand the way Jung felt about his father, one has to take notice of the exceptional closeness between them in his early years. When he was about three years old the parents were temporarily separated because of marital problems. The mother left and the father took care of the boy. This resulted in a preoedipal tie to the father that was stronger than is wholesome:

> I was sick with pseudo-croup, accompanied by choking fits. One night during an attack I stood at the foot of the bed, my head bent back over the bed rail, while my father held me under the arms. Above me I saw a glowing blue circle about the size of the full moon, and inside it moved golden figures which I thought were angels. This vision was repeated, and each time it allayed my fear of suffocation. But the suffocation returned in the anxiety dreams. I see in this a psychogenic factor: the atmosphere of the house was beginning to be unbreathable [1961, p. 18f.].

This may suffice as an illustration of his closeness to his father, who provided maternal care in lieu of the absent mother. The child's never forgiving the mother's early desertion may have shifted his reproach against her to the father, who was always generous and nonauthoritarian. Nonetheless, he was rejected by his son, who was ashamed of his father's sermons and criticized him for his religious ideas; he even doubted that his father knew what he was preaching about (p. 46f.). Despite feelings of compassion, "[a]n abyss had opened" between them (p. 55). It is a father's natural function to be wiser than his son and to lend him his wisdom for guidance, but the child reversed the relationship and pretended to know the ways of God better than his clergyman father, thereby turning inferiority into superiority, a process equivalent to his transformation of sinning into piety. The father was broadminded and enlightened enough not to insist that his son attend church regularly or take the sacraments, and yet the son repudiated him because the father accepted the church's tenets without opposition. The significance of the *Septem Sermones* is all the greater in the light of Jung's contempt for his father as a preacher.

VIII

As is to be expected, conflicts with the father were bound to appear in one way or another in Jung's relationship to Freud. Homosexual and narcissistic conflicts should be distinguished among the unconscious determinants. A harbinger of the former is visible in one of Jung's early letters, which Freud should have taken with greater seriousness than he perhaps did. In his letter of 28 October 1907, Jung had written the following, part of which was cited above:

> Actually—and I confess this to you with a struggle—I have a boundless admiration for you both as a man and a researcher, and I bear you no conscious grudge. So the self-preservation complex does not come from there; it is rather that my veneration for you has something of the character of a "religious" crush. Though it does not really bother me, I still feel it is disgusting and ridiculous because of its undeniable erotic undertone. This abominable feeling comes from the fact that as a boy I was the victim of a sexual assault by a man I once worshipped. . . . This feeling, which I still have not quite got rid of, hampers me considerably. . . . *I therefore fear your confidence.* I also fear the same reaction from you when I speak of my intimate affairs. Consequently, I skirt round such things as much as possible, for, to my feeling at any rate, every intimate relationship turns out after a while to be sentimental and banal or exhibitionistic, as with my chief [Bleuler], whose confidences are offensive [Jung's emphasis].

This, I think, is the only time that Jung averred a devastating trauma, which he had suffered as a youngster. Evidently, closeness of an idealized male who approached him with gentleness and affection aroused a bitter memory in him and fear of repetition. As will be seen, his covert feminine attitude went so far as to include pregnancy fantasies.

The homosexual conflict rose to the surface while he was on active duty as a physician in the Army:

> . . . [I] am beginning to feel squat and ugly again. Luckily I have some time for myself, so I am not

entirely pulverized by the constant spectacle of odious corporeality. Besides, something can be gained
even from its most indelicate aspect, to wit, from
what is known as the "short-arm inspection." At this
phallic parade of 500 soldiers 14% had phimosis [4
October 1911].

Male physicality, intense in Army life, made him feel
"squat and ugly."

The question will be raised whether Freud aggravated the homosexual conflict by making Jung the
crown prince and expressing his admiration, affection, tenderness and care so profusely. Indeed,
Freud felt grateful that the younger man had joined
him. At the same time—and this is something one
might have expected to reduce the conflict—Jung had
acquired a new father, who knew all the answers and
bore the halo of greatness, everything the real father
had been lacking. And still Jung did not resist the
temptation to act out aggression.

Freud's premature distribution of the patrimony
may seem like a repetition of King Lear's mistake. But
Freud was not being irrational when he desired to
relinquish administrative functions in order to concentrate on his research; the management of organi-
zational matters must have been a wearisome chore
for him. Only when, on the occasion of the Second
International Psychoanalytic Congress in Nuremberg
in 1909, Freud aspired toward permanent, absolute
power for Jung over the whole organization, is one
reminded of Lear. But it was constructive strategy to
perscrutate officially acknowledged leadership for a
charismatic, unusually talented man who had excellent publications to his credit and had proved his met-
tle in the defense of psychoanalysis at international
meetings.

Jung's covert homosexuality and his defense against it will make it possible to explain some of his bizarre behavior. There was the seemingly inexplicable switch from his letter to Freud of 26 November 1912 to the one of 3 December 1912. The first one, full of affection, written under the impact of Freud's personality when they met in Munich, and the next one, with its rudeness and vulgarity, demonstrate Jung's defense of converting homosexual attraction into its opposite.[16]

By stressing the erotic-sexual conflict, I do not want to minimize the narcissistic one, which culminated in Jung's blunt admission: "You are a dangerous rival" (14 November 1911). Gratifying as the relationship was initially for Jung, it became a thorn in his side. He had to aspire to superiority over the new father, too. The status of a crown prince means a debt to a father. I am not far off the mark when I suspect, as I have intimated, that Jung was laboring under the illusion of being the greatest mind of his century—an illusion that was in danger of being shattered if he had to bow to Freud's superiority and therefore had to share the century with his teacher.

During his early association with Freud, Jung had asked for the position of the son; he wrote (20 February 1908): "The undeserved gift of your friendship is one of the high points in my life which I cannot celebrate with big words." Circumstances impelled him "to ask you to let me enjoy your friendship not as

---

[16]The affectionate letter Jung wrote immediately after the Munich meeting may have been prompted by the close physical contact when he "carried [Freud] to a couch in the lounge" after "Freud fell on the floor in a dead faint" (Jones, 1953, p. 317). Freud's passive surrender to the strong Jung may have assuaged old rivalries, which, however, flared up again when an undefeated, vigorous Freud re-emerged in his next letter.

one between equals but as that of father and son. This distance appears to me fitting and natural. Moreover it alone, so it seems to me, strikes a note that would prevent misunderstandings and enable two hard-headed people to exist alongside one another in an easy and unstrained relationship."

Yet his awareness that Freud might be superior to him in any dimension of life became ultimately intolerable. In one of his lighter moments he acknowledged this quite freely. At a time (26 July 1911) when their friendship was on solid ground he wrote: "The feeling of inferiority that often overcomes me when I measure myself against you has always to be compensated by increased emulation." Freud tried to free him from that conflict, as Jung's letter (12 April 1909) written after a five-day visit in Vienna suggests:

> That last evening with you has, most happily, freed me inwardly from the oppressive sense of your paternal authority. My unconscious celebrated this impression with a great dream which has preoccupied me for some days and which I have just finished analysing. I hope I am now rid of all unnecessary encumbrances. Your cause must and will prosper, so my pregnancy fantasies tell me, which luckily you caught in the end.

Although this remark proves, as noted before (cf. footnote 9), that Freud's analysis of Jung went beyond dream interpretation, it is out of the question that occasional interpretations of that kind could have removed the grave conflicts that burdened Jung's relationship with a father-substitute.

In the end, Jung accused Freud of being self-righteous, of not having been analyzed, of being a tyrant, and whatnot. But this negative image evolved shortly after he had expressed great admiration. In such a short time Freud did not undergo a change of an extent that could explain Jung's final verdict. The course that his relationship with his own father had taken had to be, and was, repeated.

In his writings, too, Jung had only negative things to say about Freud, and even in his obituary article he was incapable of expressing gratitude. From his *Memories* nobody could have surmised the debt he owed Freud, the magnitude of which is revealed only in their correspondence. Gratitude was not his forte. It has been noted by several critics that in the *Memories* he mentions but once (p. 255) Eugen Bleuler—to whom he was likewise beholden—and then only as a witness of an event that was of exclusive importance to Jung himself. Only Philemon was acknowledged with gratitude as a paternal authority; Jung could bow without ambivalence to a father whom he himself had created. This, in turn, concealed the wish to be his own father (cf. Freud, 1910, p. 173), which, I am certain, was quite strong in Jung and contributed to his hostility against father images.

IX

Jung's break with Freud did not provide the blessing he had expected from a state of freedom. The dilemma he was facing in a life without Freud was almost graver than the one he had faced in a life with him, and this forced him to resort to radical solutions. One of them was the denial of the root conflicts in the personal unconscious, and with it the depth of the personal unconscious in general. He obstructed psychology and made the dogma of the collective unconscious the fundamental principle of analytical psychology. The crushing burden of having cursed the Holy Spirit left only one escape route: God was the creator of all things and therefore also of such a blasphemy. But God cannot be invoked "in vain."

> A collective problem, if not recognized as such, always appears as a personal problem, and in individual cases may give the impression that something is out of order in the realm of the personal psyche. The personal sphere is indeed disturbed, but such disturbances need not be primary . . . [Jung, 1961, pp. 233–234].

Instead of taking responsibility for one's own unconscious, it is shifted to the collective unconscious. The person is exculpated by carrying only "secondary" responsibility, the primary one having moved outside the borders of one's subjective territory.

In carrying out this process, he had to return to an even more dangerous dogma. In his own words, "a dogma, that is to say, an undisputable confession of faith, is set up only when the aim is to suppress doubts once and for all. But that no longer has anything to do with scientific judgment; only with a personal power drive" (p. 150). Was he aware that his own work after the break with Freud was based on the dogma of God? For him, the "experience of God, [was] the most evident of all experiences." He knew "that knowledge of this sort could not be proved," but he was equally convinced "that it stood in no more need of proof than the beauty of a sunset . . ." (p. 92). "Why do these philosophers pretend that

God is an idea, a kind of arbitrary assumption which they can engender or not, when it is perfectly plain that He exists, as plain as a brick that falls on your head?" (p. 62). Verily, strange things were falling from heaven to prove God's existence: once, a huge piece of excrement, then, a brick; did Jung *ever* stop sinning against the Holy Spirit?

Freud the atheist, the materialist, the positivist and whatnot had to be inferior to the God-fearing pastor's son. But in one respect Freud was undeniably superior to Jung: his sexual record was lily-white. His theory, of course, was obscene, with its eternal harping on sex, but the conduct of the man who originated it was beyond reproach. It must have disquieted Jung that the Jew Freud should have been more moral than the Christian-Gentile-Nordic Jung; for even though he may have hoped that the Spielrein affair had been forgotten, another cloud of impurity had gathered: he was in the process of initiating a relationship that would, without divorce from his wife, lead to a second marriage with Antonia Wolff (1888–1953). At least that was the way he characterized the arrangement, according to a memoir whose authorship I am not free to disclose. As stated by that source, Jung felt like an African chieftain with two wives—which, of course, was something that would not have made Philemon happy, but then, even the Holy Spirit had forgiven Jung. The arrangement, Jung insisted, was a true trinity, the second woman coming into the relationship on an equal status with the woman of the house. After all, he had maintained in a letter to Freud (30 January 1910) that "[t]he prerequisite for a good marriage, it seems to me, is the license to be unfaithful."

Possibly Antonia Wolff's appearance in Zurich precipitated the break with Freud. Her name came up only once in their correspondence, when Jung enumerated the women who would participate in the Weimar Congress, among them " . . . a new discovery of mine, Frl. Antonia Wolff, a remarkable intellect with an excellent feeling for religion and philosophy," and concluded his list—ominously, one might think—with "last but not least, my wife" (29 August 1911). No sign of a weakening of his friendship with Freud was notable at that time. Just the opposite: one finds in the same letter one of Jung's strongest statements of praise of Freud and again a declaration of his place as a son. In response to Freud's words of thanks and praise in recognition of the last issue of the *Jahrbuch*, Jung replied that he "was overjoyed" by Freud's letter, "being, as you know, very receptive to any recognition the father sees fit to bestow." He had "the feeling that this is a time full of marvels, and, if the augures do not deceive us, it may very well be that, thanks to your discoveries, we are on the threshold of something really sensational, which I scarcely know how to describe except with the Gnostic concept of *sophia*, an Alexandrian term particularly suited to the reincarnation of ancient wisdom in the shape of psychoanalysis."

At that time, then, his friendship with Freud bore no trace of impending disturbance; but only a little more than a year later, in November 1912, Jung's behavior had changed to such a degree that Freud felt forced to switch from his usual address of "Dear Friend" to "Lieber Herr Doktor" (Dear Dr. Jung). During that period Jung had traveled to the United States, and there was a gap from 2 August 1912 to 11

November 1912, during which he did not send a single letter. He also had spent little time with his wife. She wrote Freud (10 September 1912, see McGuire, 1974):

> Carl was away nearly all summer; since Saturday he has been on the trip to America after spending only one day here between military service and departure. I have so much to do now that I can't let too much libido travel after him to America, it might so easily get lost on the way.

The possibility cannot be excluded that he fell in love with Antonia Wolff during the very first year of their acquaintance. This would have been in keeping with his confession to Sabina Spielrein years earlier (4 December 1908) that "[i]t is my misfortune that I cannot for my life forgo the bliss of love, tempestuous, forever changing love" (Carotenuto, 1986, p. 196). The reader will recall that he expected a "dressing down" from Freud for his involvement with Spielrein, admitting that it was stupid that Freud's "son and heir" should squander Freud's heritage. Just as in 1908, he might not have succeeded in keeping his renewed unfaithfulness a secret and Emma Jung might easily have turned to Freud. Such embarrassing events had to be forestalled.

But Jung's liaison with Antonia Wolff was necessary, if for no other reason than as an emergency measure. Again according to the informant, Jung had recognized that his life was upset and his work had become hampered. Antonia Wolff did not live in Jung's home, but she was part of his household. The informant watched both women prepare dinner when he visited Küsnacht, and wondered at the pain and torture that Emma Jung must have suffered as a result of her husband's unfaithfulness. That Emma was unhappy in her marriage prior to her husband's relationship with Antonia Wolff is known from a letter to Freud (24 November 1911).[17] It sounds hardly believable but, according to the informant, Jung told him that he got Emma to take Latin lessons to channel her energies into constructive paths. (Let us hope she did not come across Ovid's *Ars amatoria*.) The happiness of Jung's children did not remain unscathed by this domestic setup, and the informant raised the question of whether it might not have been better for Emma Jung to divorce her husband. Whatever the answer, he was sure that Jung would have lost his creativeness without Antonia Wolff.

The informant made a suggestion that deserves a closer look. He claimed that the physical relationship between Jung and Antonia Wolff started only after 1920. Although this claim was based on grounds that are not convincing, it struck me that, as Jung reported, between 1918 and 1920 he found "stability, and gradually my inner peace returned" (Jung, 1961, p. 197). This would mean that the malignant process that had started around the time of his break with Freud gradually came to an end around 1920, and eventually resulted in his gaining strength and stability enough to start a sexual relationship with the woman he loved.

The informant admired Jung for following bravely and openly the idea of the two-equal-wives system, despite his own rejection of it as a viable pattern. After Jung's trip to India (1938) and the ensuing years

---

[17]Published in McGuire, 1974, p. 467.

of his intermittent sicknesses, the informant observed, the martial relationship strengthened and the relation with Antonia Wolff became more distant, to the point where Jung could become very cutting and hurtful to her. When Wolff died in 1953, Jung wrote the informant about how shocked and at a loss he felt; and when his wife died in 1955, he was devastated. Apparently Jung felt remorse toward both women. Antonia Wolff had assets that Emma Jung did not possess. She helped Jung with his visions, whereas Emma gave him warmth and affection; but both assisted in his practice and he referred patients to both of them.

The doubts hearsay evidence deserves notwithstanding, Jung's relationship with Antonia Wolff and the details here reported throw a new light on the Billinsky interview. The Spielrein episode apart, it sounds preposterous to hear an aged man who had lived with two wives for decades describe the intensity of an agony that had seized him 50 years earlier, when he was allegedly told that his revered teacher enjoyed intimacy with a sister-in-law living in his household. Even more incredible is his claim that he had never been able to forgive his teacher for that moral transgression and therefore had ultimately broken off their association.

To understand these falsifications, one has to recall Jung's need to emulate Freud whenever he perceived an inferiority in himself, as he described it in the letter of 26 July 1911 quoted above. Indeed, he outdid Freud in almost all respects. He evoked in the cultural community the image and fame of being a seer; he formed his own school; he traveled throughout the world, giving innumerable interviews; and his articles were published in important journals. He also was wealthier than Freud, owned a house, and had a tower built into which he withdrew in order to meditate. His popularity was considerable and possibly exceeded Freud's, who did not see one single ghost in all his life and was never guided by a guru, nor did he ever attract spirits from Jerusalem.

But there was one area in which Jung failed even to equal Freud, much as he may have wanted to do so. When he met Freud and his wife he must have sensed, at least in Freud, the afterglow of a unique and passionate love adventure. It is my impression, if not conviction, that Freud throughout his life was grateful to fate, as well as to Martha, that his extraordinary passion for her and his unspeakable anguish of 4½ years of courtship, which had seemed hopeless, had been crowned by a triumphant consummation. Of course, the acute passion had subsided when Jung met Freud for the first time, but the lasting glow of past years of passionate love must still have existed. What is more, this glow probably encompassed both Freud and Martha, as can be inferred from her moving letter to Ludwig Binswanger (7 November 1939), in which she thanked him for his condolences on her husband's death, and adds, ". . . . in the fifty-three years of our married life not one angry word fell between us" (Binswanger, 1957, p. 102). I am inclined to believe her.

Jung may have been aware of, and responsive to, Freud's treasure of rapt recollections of a kind of which Jung's memory was void; for Jung was a consummate egotist, as is revealed in the chapter "Retrospect" in his *Memories.* He put himself into the place of a genius from whom the world cannot expect what is expected from the average mortal. "The difference," he stated, "between most people and myself is that for me the 'dividing walls' are transparent. That is my peculiarity" (Jung, 1961, p. 355). Throughout his life people came and went without leaving traces "as soon as I had seen through them" (p. 357). He attributed this to being the captive of his creative daimon, but was it not rather a trait of his character? A contemporary who knew him when both were little boys remembered him "because I had never come across such an asocial monster before" (McGuire and Hull, 1977, p. 3).

But if he could not emulate Freud as a past lover, present faithful husband and exemplary paterfamilias, at least he could destroy that image of Freud by claiming that Freud had maintained an extramarital affair from early on and, worse yet, an incestuous one. At that moment a balance was established, and even with a nuance in Jung's favor, to boot. However, his remark to Billinsky, "If Freud would have tried to understand consciously the triangle [i.e., would have had complete analysis], he would have been much, much better off" (Billinsky, 1969, p. 42), was not only arrogant and supercilious but also misleading. Freud was fortunate and extremely happy with his family. There he found everything he needed. Beside providing the warmth and affection of which he was always desirous, his family also allowed for the quietness of evening hours that he could devote undistractedly to his writing. No serious conflict between him and his wife or his children is known. No domestic obstacles stood in the way of the unfolding of his genius. His self-analysis had also carried him to deeper depths than his therapy of Jung, for he acknowledged, at age

62, his death-wish for his eldest son (Freud, 1900, pp. 558–560) without going into a frenzy of suicidal impulses.

X

Coming to the end of my exploration, I believe I have proved that Minna Bernays never confided the secret of an intimate relationship with her brother-in-law to Jung. This much is unquestionable. Whether Freud actually entertained such a relationship can only be gauged with reference to probabilities. That he was deeply attached to Minna Bernays and held her in high esteem is evident from his letters to Fliess and from the testimonies of other witnesses. If Freud had had a mistress living in his home, he might be called reckless, since young daughters were growing up in the family and were expected to live up to the strict moral precepts that governed their parents' lives.

If further research[18] should unearth proof of an intimate relationship between Freud and Minna Bernays,

[18]The publication of the Freud-Minna Bernays correspondence, to the extent that it has been preserved, might help to decide the question of whether Freud entertained an intimate relationship with his sister-in-law. More than 70 letters from Freud to Minna Bernays, and 80 of her letters to him, are deposited in the Library of Congress. Peter Gay (1989) examined those that are unrestricted and found nothing indicative of intimacy. Anna Freud made me the custodian of the restricted letters and I have released them to Dr. Albrecht Hirschmüller, who is ready to edit them as soon as arrangements have been made for publication.

There seems to be no question that some letters from this correspondence are missing. Ernst Freud told me that Minna Bernays requested the destruction of the letters Freud wrote her; whether she meant to include her letters as well, I do not know. Evidently her request was not carried out, at least not completely. The Freud family was negligent in the care of Freud's letters. Some of them—and I recall that a few of these were addressed to Minna Bernays—were kept in an unlocked closet in a corridor of Anna Freud's house. Thus, there were opportu-

this would necessitate a revision of the ideas that have been held about Freud. His puritanism would not have been as firm as is believed, and the degree of internalization of conflict he supposedly had achieved would have been overrated. What speaks against such a relationship is the testimony of everyone who had contact with the Freuds as to the family's striking harmony, geniality and cheerful spirits. It stands to reason that this cannot be expected if the father is maintaining an illicit affair in the household. Karl Marx did it, but he had a notoriously bad marriage, an illegitimate son, and two daughters who committed suicide. None of Freud's children suffered from an unusually intense psychopathology that would pre-suppose a family background torn by conflict.

What Jung told Billinsky was, for the largest part, a projection; the following will illustrate one element of it. Lewis Mumford (1968, p. 39) reported that he saw three large photographs on a wall of the Jung Institute in Zurich, which were removed shortly thereafter: "To the left was an elderly woman with a strongly modelled face and slightly grim, almost formidable. . . . In the center was Dr. Jung, in ripe old age. . . . The third was a somewhat younger woman, finely modelled, self-possessed, . . . more the face of a pure intellectual than Jung's."

The striking feature of Mumford's description of the two women is that it comes so close to what Jung told Billinsky about Freud's wife and Minna Bernays. As the reader will remember, Martha Freud was in-troduced as an elderly wife, and Minna Bernays as

---

nities for loss. However, the main reason letters are missing seems to be Minna Bernays's request reported above.

"very good-looking." However, at the time Jung arrived in Vienna, Martha Freud was still good-looking
and retained something of the appearance that had
made her so attractive to Freud, whereas Minna's
appearance was matronlike and rather bare of attraction, as can be learned from contemporary photographs. Antonia Wolff has been described as strik-
ingly beautiful.

This essay may be of importance in a more general
sense. It proves how carefully one has to weigh the
depositions of witnesses. Some historians act accord-
ingly and ask *cui bono?* If the testimony is detrimental,
or at least not of advantage to the witness, they are
inclined to look at it as authentic. In Jung's interview
everything he said about Freud was to his own advantage and highly detrimental to Freud. On the other
hand, in his *Memories* he freely admitted to having
lied to Freud (Jung, 1961, p. 160), to having deceived
a patient by informing on him, behind his back, to
the patient's mother (p. 121f.), and to having told an
untruth to his dying father (p. 96). He might have
been able to rationalize the last two incidents, but it
is plain that he was not a paragon of veracity, and
therefore it is a problem why, in the absence of compelling necessity, he confessed mendacity toward
Freud, a type of action people usually deny or re-
press.

* * * * *

Who is believed: the deceiver or the truth seeker?
is a question many a reader may have asked. The
answer probably varies with the subject to which the
deceiver devotes his effort and the climate of the
times. Nowadays, someone who seeks to detract

Freud has an edge over the truth seeker, as an example will illustrate. Jeffrey M. Masson made a name for himself over the whole world with a book, *Assault on Truth: Freud's Suppression of the Seduction Theory* (1984). In that work Masson tried to prove that Freud, against his better knowledge, replaced his original theory of seduction (1896), which had gotten him into disrepute in Vienna, with that of infantile sexuality (1905).

Masson's book contains no proof that has a bearing on the seduction theory except for an unpublished document that he had come across accidentally, the content of which, as reported by him, was highly detrimental to Freud with regard to the question of Freud's motives for giving up the seduction theory. When I gained access to the unpublished document, it was obvious that it did not contain anything of the sort Masson had claimed.

I mention this for a particular reason. On the Op-Ed page of *The New York Times* of April 22, 1991, there appeared an article by Masson that contained the following statement:

> The best way to safeguard scholarship is to encourage the liberal use of accurate quotations. An inexact quotation from an unpublished source may remain invisible for years, causing great harm.[19]

I thought it appropriate to send a letter to the editor comparing, side by side, what Masson had published as the content of the unpublished document and

---

[19]It is, of course, nonsense to maintain that an inexact quotation from an unpublished source may remain *invisible* for years. A quotation, exact or inexact, is always visible. The thought that caused that parapraxis in his thinking probably was to this effect: May the unpublished source of my inexact quotation remain invisible for years.

what it actually said. My letter was rejected. When Freud calumniators are protected so effectively, the reading public can hardly be expected to obtain a correct image of what kind of a man Freud really was.

The deceiver's pen is usually persuasive. He writes with passion and gives himself the standing of the only honest person in a world of deceit and trumpery. Many equivalents to the superiority of the deceiver's pen can be found. Parents are often chagrined when their children show every inclination to imitate their weaknesses but rarely their probity. In other words, vice is more attractive than virtue. My teacher August Aichhorn explained the phenomenon by the general rule that children are drawn to parental attributes that are ensconced in passions, rather than to others; we may be certain that parents invest more feelings into their vices than into their virtues. The deceiver often writes with greater compelling force than the truth seeker, who prefers to let truth speak for itself. Only after a period of time, long as it may be, is the deceiver unmasked, usually when the subject matter has moved to the periphery of interest. The very few who are still mindful of the matter can then only say, *Requiescat in pace.*

REFERENCES

Billinsky, J. M. (1969), Jung and Freud (The end of a romance). *Andover-Newton Quarterly,* 10:39–43.

Binswanger, L. (1957), *Sigmund Freud: Reminiscences of a Friendship,* trans. by Norbert Guterman. New York: Grune and Stratton.

Carotenuto, A. (1982), *A Secret Symmetry. Sabina Spielrein between Jung and Freud,* trans. by Arno Pomerans, John Shepley, & Krishna Winston. New York: Pantheon Books.

—— ed. (1986), *Tagebuch einer heimlichen Symmetrie. Sabina Spielrein zwischen Jung und Freud.* Editor's essay trans. Dorothea Agerer. Freiburg i. Br.: Kore.

Choisy, M. (1971), *Mes Enfances Mémoires, 1903–1924.* Geneva: Mont Blanc.

Eissler, K. R. (1982), *Psychologische Aspekte des Briefwechsels zwischen Freud und Jung.* Jahrbuch der Psychoanalyse, Beiheft 7. Stuttgart-Bad Canstatt: Frommann-holzbog.

—— (in press), Some misconceptualizations and paramnesias in J. M. Masson's publications on Freud's seduction theory. *Psychoanalytic Quarterly.*

Ellenberger, H. (1970), *The Discovery of the Unconscious: The History and Evolution of Dynamic Psychiatry.* New York: Basic Books.

Freud, M. (1957), *Glory Reflected: Sigmund Freud, Man and Father.* London: Angus and Robertson.

Freud, S. (1900), The Interpretation of Dreams. *Standard Edition,* 4-5. London: Hogarth Press, 1953.

—— (1905), Three essays on the theory of sexuality. *Standard Edition,* 7:135–243. London: Hogarth Press, 1953.

—— (1910), A special type of choice of object made by men. *Standard Edition,* 11:165–175. London: Hogarth Press, 1957.

—— (1914), On narcissism: An introduction. *Standard Edition,* 14:69–102. London: Hogarth Press, 1957.

—— (1937), Analysis terminable and interminable. *Standard Edition,* 23:216–253. London: Hogarth Press, 1964.

—— (1960a), *Letters of Sigmund Freud,* ed. Ernst L. Freud, trans. Tania and James Stern. New York: Basic Books.

—— (1960[1923]), Sigmund Freud and G. Stanley Hall: Exchange of letters. *Psychoanal. Quart.,* 29:307–316.

Gay, P. (1988), *Freud: A Life for Our Time.* New York: W. W. Norton.

—— (1989), Sigmund and Minna? The biographer as voyeur. *New York Times Book Review,* January 29, 1989.

Groesbeck, C. J. (1980), The analyst's myth. Freud and Jung as each other's analyst. *Quadrant,* Journal of the C. G. Jung Foundation for Analytic Psychology, Spring Issue: 28–55.

Jones, E. (1953), *The Life and Work of Sigmund Freud,* Vol. 1. New York: Basic Books.

—— (1955), *The Life and Work of Sigmund Freud,* Vol. 2. New York: Basic Books.

Jung, C. G. (1916), *Psychology of the Unconscious,* trans. Beatrice M. Hinkle, of *Wandlungen und Symbole der Libido* (1912). New York: Moffat, Yard and Co.

—— (1961), *Memories, Dreams, Reflections.* Recorded and edited by Aniela Jaffé, trans. by Richard & Clara Winston. New York: Pantheon Books.

———— (1976), *The Collected Works,* vol. 18, The Symbolic Life. Miscellaneous Writings, trans. R. F. C. Hull. Princeton, NJ: Princeton University Press (Bollingen Series XX).

———— (1989), *Analytical Psychology.* Notes of the Seminar Given in Zurich in 1925. Edited by William McGuire. Princeton, NJ: Princeton University Press.

Masson, J. M. (1984), *Assault on Truth: Freud's Suppression of the Seduction Theory.* New York: Penguin Books.

McGuire, W., ed. (1974), *The Freud/Jung Letters,* trans. Ralph Manheim & R. F. C. Hull. Princeton, NJ: Princeton University Press (Bollingen Series, XCIV).

———— R. F. C. Hull, eds. (1977), *C. G. Jung Speaking. Interviews and Encounters.* Princeton, NJ: Princeton University Press (Bollingen Series XCVII).

Mumford, L. (1968), Reflections: European Diary. *The New Yorker,* July 6, 1968.

Ostow, M. (1977), Letter to the Editor. *Internat. Rev. Psycho-Anal.,* 4:377.

Stargardt, J. A., Autograph Auction House, Catalogue No. 608 (n.d.). Marburg, Germany.

THE MALIGNED THERAPIST OR, AN UNSOLVED PROBLEM OF PSYCHOANALYTIC TECHNIQUE

In the analysis of a young woman who became famous in the history of psychoanalysis under the name of Dora, Freud (1905) discovered, in 1900, the momentous importance of the emotional relationship to the analyst that the patient creates in his unconscious. Freud called it transference when he discovered that what appeared clinically as being genuine was in truth transferred from other sources. He found that the transference relationship was determined by a compromise among a variety of forces, the most significant of which were not referable to the analyst's personality and behavior but were of extraneous origin. Primarily, they originated in the patient's life history, starting in earliest infancy, as well as in unconscious imagery involving the analyst, fantasies, along with loving and aggressive impulses that were

This chapter is an expanded and improved version of a paper originally published in German under the title "Der Verleumdete Therapist—über Ein Ungelöstes Problem der Psychoanalytischer Tecknik," *Jahrbuch der Psychoanalyse*, 27:9–28, 1991. It has been published in the *Journal of Clinical Psychoanalysis*, 2:175–217, 1993.

formed in accordance with past experiences and were often almost replicas of them. Transference and the technique of how it should be handled moved into the center of psychoanalytic clinical and research interests. Through its observation the therapist became acquainted with the deepest layers of the patient's repressed. The knowledge thus acquired, when skillfully applied, helped achieve the optimal outcome of therapy.

In the course of an analysis, the analysand transmits to the analyst, to the extent that he can, the full range of his inner world; during treatment sessions the analyst in turn, concentrating on the subject's world, becomes totally absorbed in it to the exclusion of all other concerns. This mental closeness of analyst and analysand permits one to call their relationship a dyad, which serves its purpose optimally when the image of the analyst that is brought into the analysis is given shape principally, if not exclusively, by the analysand's imagination.

In order to secure a transference that is minimally affected by the analyst's reality, the patient should know as little as possible about the analyst. Therefore, the patient's actual knowledge of the therapist is kept to the unavoidable minimum. The analyst then comes close to serving as a tabula rasa, like a flawless mirror whose perfection guarantees an undistorted replication of an image—in this instance, the image the patient has molded of the therapist in accordance with his past and with his fantasies. By spending the treatment session supine, unable to see the analyst, the patient, through free association and interpretation, gradually is made aware of the image he has formed of the analyst and the incidents of the past that lay dormant behind it.

However, not only the patient's past life experiences but also, as said above, his fantasies and imagery about the therapist engendered in the present find their way into the transference. Often, these fantasies are attached to, and therefore hide behind, observations and knowledge he has gained about the therapist's reality: I shall refer to associations of the latter type as amounting to a "contamination of transference," meaning that they are not only derivatives of the patient's repressed inner world but also reflect the actual and fantasized reality of the analytic environment.

An analyst's office, the way he dresses, moves, speaks and gestures, everything becomes the vehicle of the therapist's personal traits and tastes. The patient will, consciously and unconsciously, build an image of the analyst that to varying degrees contains both subjective features and aspects of reality, as well as derivatives of each.[1]

My use of the term "contamination" may sound like a warning, as if I recommended that the patient be treated in a sterile environment, empty of any impression of his therapist and the therapist's habitat. In reality, a sterile transference would never lead to optimal results. The daily observations the patient makes regarding the analyst generally serve as stimuli to the formation of transference and, when properly analyzed, contribute in the vast majority of instances

---

[1]Clinically, one observes two extremes: those few patients who achieve a surprisingly correct picture of the analyst's person, and those who appear insensitive and do not seem to notice anything idiosyncratic in the analyst and his habitat.

to the advancement of treatment.[2] In this essay I shall first briefly survey sources of contamination and then concentrate on a category of knowledge about the therapist which the patient acquired from the outside and which may, though under rare circumstances, lead to a contamination that could seriously endanger a favorable course of treatment. In doing so, however, I do not mean to moderate the above caveat regarding sterile transference.

I

Analysts differ in their efforts to meet the factor of contamination. Some handle that problem with liberality; they do not mind, indeed occasionally even favor, social contacts with their patients outside the treatment situation. At the opposite extreme is the analyst who, as has been alleged, resorts to the bizarre technique of demanding that his patients enter and leave the treatment room without looking at him.

It would be an interesting experiment to create a situation in which only minimal contamination of transference can occur. What course would a treatment take if the patient were prevented from ever coming face to face with the analyst—that is, if the therapist's identity remained unknown to the patient from the beginning and contacts were limited to interpretations? Such a setup could be arranged in a psychoanalytic outpatient clinic, with the analyst sitting

---

[2]Freud warned against manipulation of transference for the purpose of evoking conflicts (Freud, 1937, pp. 230–233). "Natural" and artificially provoked, avoidable transference are sometimes difficult to keep apart in clinical practice.

behind a one-way screen. Or the dehumanization could be carried even a step further by having interpretations appear typed out on a screen. Both eventualities would be Kafkaesque and should, according to psychoanalytic tenets, lead to therapeutic failure, the patient being thrust more and more toward a paranoid dilemma.

Transference, with all the conflicts it will arouse in the patient, and with the contingent technical difficulties of handling and interpreting it, aggravated by countertransference—which, according to its present definition, is unavoidable[3]—may be judged as a nuisance that ought to be avoided. This may lead some to look at the therapist's total elimination as an appropriate goal. Technology indeed makes human skills unnecessary. Soon high-school youngsters armed with their computers will be able to defeat a boastful whilom chess champion. The intrusion of the computer into psychotherapy and ultimately into psychoanalysis is becoming a realistic danger. Selmi et al. (1990) recommend computerized therapy, for to them it is superior to human efforts. The computerized therapist never is cranky, never has bad days, and though he always listens, he demands no more than a fee of 50 cents per session. In mild to moderate depressions, these authors are certain, computerized therapy is as efficient as human therapeutic effort. I

---

[3]In Freud's usage of the term, countertransference is avoidable. He limited the concept to those emotional reactions in the therapist which lead to an impairment of psychoanalytic technique (Freud, 1910, 1915). However, he wrote to an early collaborator who got into trouble by falling in love with a patient, "But no lasting harm is done. [Such experiences] help us to develop the thick skin we need and to dominate 'countertransference,' which is after all a permanent problem for us; they teach us to displace our own affects to best advantage. They are a *blessing in disguise* " (Freud to Jung on June 6, 1909; McGuire, 1974, p. 145).

should add to their recommendations that among all its virtues, the computer's incomparable memory is by no means a minor one. One awaits the day when, because of the dearth of priests, the computer will also be met in the confessional.

Yet, extreme and unusual situations aside, within the transference neuroses the optimal prompting and stimulating of transference does not require social exchanges, nor is it to be feared and shunned. Despite the many peculiarities of the psychoanalytic situation, such as its unequal and lopsided basis, it is, au fond, not unnatural: it leads to contacts of extraordinary intensity between two people that are incompatible with a mechanical gap of emptiness, such as a computer would entail; it presupposes the presence of two live human beings. To be sure, the optimal intensity may vary with the patient's personality and disorder. Depressive personalities may need more stimulation, and a euphoric temperament more distance than the average person. I shall not pursue the challenging question of the correct proportion between stimulation and distance, but shall return to a brief consideration of ways in which objective information about the therapist's reality may contaminate transference.

II

I shall enumerate in loose sequence a variety of eventualities. Patients are frequently given objective clues regarding the analyst's marital status and children when the therapist's professional and private premises are the same. Many patients obtain that knowledge one way or another. Status symbols, such as the office address, afford knowledge of the therapist's standing in the profession, or his aspirations. The fee per se communicates something about the therapist's attitude toward money. One patient showed great ingenuity in testing his therapist's sense of acquisition and hoarding: he observed the time the therapist let lapse between receipt and deposit of his checks. He kept his test a secret for years, the result of his test having a profound effect on his transference. The illusion that the number of publications and offices held in professional organizations permit an estimate of the therapist's clinical qualifications is widespread, and it can be taken for granted that the patient's interest in such particulars will rarely attenuate until he has acquired this information.

Nowadays many patients ask, in the pretreatment interview, for details of the analyst's training and want to know which "school of therapy" the therapist "believes in." By checking rosters and professional directories, patients usually inform themselves about the therapist's age and schooling before they make their first appointment. I heard of a patient who went from one therapist to another in search of one who would answer all his questions, some of which concerned rather personal details, a demand he justified by the necessity of knowing the person to whom he was expected to entrust his secrets. When at last he found a cooperating analyst and was ready to start treatment, he was given the correct interpretation that his request was an acting-out aimed at forestalling the treatment by obstructing a spontaneous evolvement of transference. This practical demonstration made it possible for the patient to start analysis without insisting on that bizarre beginning.

Pronounced contamination is produced if the analyst becomes pregnant (Bassen, 1988). The patient's awareness of the analyst's condition will have serious consequences for the transference and the course of treatment. It stands to reason that this contingency will touch upon problems attached to the deepest infantile conflicts, which will become activated earlier than would have occurred otherwise. Likewise, a death in the analyst's family may come to the patient's notice by reason of the widespread habit, not to say compulsion, of studying the obituary page.

I am obliged to Dr. Eva Rosenfeld for an example of outside information that might readily have led to a distressing outcome, as she told me. She moved in Freud's circle and was in training analysis with him. By accident she learned that Freud was a victim of a new outbreak of cancer of which he had not been apprised. She went to her next session in great consternation and only after a long struggle brought herself to the point of telling Freud what was troubling her. Luckily it turned out that Freud was not oblivious of his condition. (For a different version of this episode see Jones, 1957, p. 153.) This instance, unusual though it was, nevertheless points to the possibility that a patient may possess information that is vital to the analyst and yet unknown to him.

Another source of outside information is dependent upon the therapist's position in the community. If an analyst is prominent in a political or other movement, or if he is mentioned in the media, the patient's transference will be heavily tinged by knowledge obtained from these sources.

Anna Freud once remarked that a patient's possession of objective knowledge about the therapist makes his analysis all the more difficult. She certainly did not have knowledge of peripheral data and details in mind but rather knowledge of the kind Max Schur reported about her in his book on Freud. In 1938, when escape from Vienna seemed impossible for the Freud family, she asked her father, "Wouldn't it be better if we all killed ourselves?," to which Freud replied, "Why? Because they would like us to?" (Schur, 1972, p. 499). Evidently this incident was meant to illustrate Freud's way of thinking, and it would have been sufficient to report that one of his children had asked the question, which would have spared Anna Freud the anguish she must have felt repeatedly when her patients reminded her of that tragic episode.

The detrimental effect of knowledge about the therapist when acquired from outside sources, and not from personal observation, must have played an enormous role in Freud's training analyses. The analysands' access to the abundance of biographical data spread throughout his publications created the unique situation in which the analysand knew more than was good for him about his analyst. Analyses of trainees are per se more difficult to conduct than those of patients; that Freud's analyses of candidates so frequently required continuation with others may have resulted in part from the subject's knowledge of the analyst's psychopathology.

III

I have not mentioned all possible types of contamination, but to do so is unnecessary since the purpose of this communication is to discuss a specific one, one that may compromise transference gravely and, as can be imagined, under unfavorable conditions even injure it irreparably. This comes into play when the patient happens to acquire information harmful to his therapist's reputation. The effect of such information on the patient, aside from its content, will depend also on whether it is trivial gossip or vilification, and whether it was orally transmitted or in print.

Gossip and rumor are psychosocial phenomena deserving attention and yet have rarely been subjects of psychoanalytic investigation. Inasmuch as they serve as sources of biographical material, they ought to be of interest to historians and psychologists. They are indicators of covert processes that have surrounded a biographer's subject and, more frequently than not, have resulted in notable effects.

Gossip may appear in various forms. As a political rumor it may have momentous consequences, particularly at times of weakened societal cohesion, a topic beyond the scope of this essay. In private life, one has to differentiate between hard-core—that is, malicious—and soft-core gossip. At times, the former has grave consequences; the latter is widespread but more or less inconsequential on the societal level.

Psychoanalytic common sense can, with little effort, reconstruct some of the processes that drive habitual, gossipy detractors like a pack of hounds in relentless pursuit of their often helpless prey. The usual assortment of unconscious constellations that are operative when man does that which he ought not to do can be expected to be activated to varying degree and extent in persons who have become addicted to gossiping. In their analyses one may expect to observe: defenses against, and gratification of, paranoid and homosexual impulses and fantasies; illusions of omnipotence; cannibalistic impulses; the triumph of soiling in public; the denial of the gossiper's own defects, and their projection, compensation and revenge for infantile frustrations and humiliations; and jealousy, envy, and vindictiveness—actions which, when typical of an individual, betoken a narcissistic, exhibitionistic, destructive character organization. A self-destructive impulse in the detractor should not be overlooked for it is operative with greater frequency than one would expect. A writer who had an uncanny ability to induce the subjects of her interviews to make unintentionally self-damaging statements succeeded in one instance in amassing a collection of highly compromising confessions. In one of her publications she included, without any ostensible necessity, a few statements that her victim had never made. She was so unwise as to put them in quotation marks—that sacred stamp of absolute veracity—which got her into trouble. Those remarks had been supererogatorily added to an otherwise excellent and accurate piece.

This avoidable, unwarranted self-destructive gesture affords a glimpse into the denigrator's masochistic tie to the object of her attack. She provoked her target by testing the limits of his tolerance. It seemed in that instance as if the exploiter had a secret hankering to be exploited in turn by the one she had exploited. It is well known that the victim identifies with the aggressor, but the aggressor may identify with the victim. A covert mutuality connects the one who causes suffering and the one who is exposed to it.

There are also those for whom gossip is a kind of benign hobby and who tell tales just for the sake of doing so, without thought of scheming and plotting and, when viewed superficially, without malicious intent.

Gossip satisfies a group desire that in general is insatiable, demanding to be fed ever-renewed tidbits; society and gossipmongers are linked by a bond of reciprocal stimulation. Again, a kind of complementary relationship is discernible.

Soft-core gossip commonly does not reach print and constitutes, in its daily appearance, an informal, "off the record" network of communication among members of a group. Yet, as noted, although it primarily provides the detractor with an outlet for his free-floating aggression, the detractor may nevertheless inadvertently fulfill an important function: by virtue of a potential wrongdoer's fear lest he himself become victimized by denigration, gossip serves to warn against transgressions and reduce their frequency.

Gossip creates a covert world of its own, usually anonymous and informal. It comes and goes, sometimes causing a short-lasting flurry, but usually being quickly discarded by the listener. Othello's famous lines, "He that filches from me my good name . . . makes me poor," may indeed be valid in some instances, but as a rule a person is not even aware of the gossip of which his imputed acts form the content, and what was said about him reaches him, if at all, by accident years later, when it has lost its acute flavor. It even is a matter of good manners to maintain that secrecy; to mention gossip and rumors in the presence of the target is considered aggressive. "One does not refer to the rope in the house of the hanged man," is a cognate concern in the vernacular of some languages. In short, the gossipmonger and his audience enjoy delectable tidbits about a third party, who is often unaware of providing occasion for such enjoyment.[4]

The social situation of the person maligned by gossip is the inverse of that in the typical dream of nakedness or undress (Freud, 1900, pp. 242–248). The dreamer is aware that his attire is deficient and feels intensely ashamed, but other people in the dream take no notice of the defect. In the case of gossip, however, everyone except the victim is aware of the flaws in the latter's image.

On the other hand, the dream of nakedness and the social reality of gossip have in common that in both situations external appearances remain unruffled. Nothing in the manifest dream reflects the agitation in which the dreamer finds himself in the dream of nakedness. Likewise, the social atmosphere surrounding the person gossiped about usually remains unaffected even when obnoxious detractions are circulating. Another feature shared by dreamer and gossiper is hypocrisy. The dreamer covertly enjoys exhibitionistic pleasure while feeling excessively virtuous shame. A gossiper who has started or heard a scandalous slander will, upon meeting the disparaged

---

[4]I do not consider the institutionalization of gossip in the form of tabloids and columns in magazines and newspapers.

person, act as if the slander did not exist, but he will pass it on as a fact at the next opportunity. Emotions, however, are, so to speak, complementary in the dreams and in gossip: the dreamer's excessive embarrassment finds its counterpart in the gossiper's voyeuristic pleasure in exposing a subject's alleged imperfections to the stare of his contemporaries.

As is all too well known, gossip does not always take an innocuous course and may even have tragic consequences, in conformity with Othello's famous utterance. In the biblical Suzanne's case, gossip might have led to her execution if divine intervention had not saved her. The slanderers had accused her of having done the very thing they had in vain attempted to do to her. Election campaigns of our times deserve mention here; they are events in which vilification is entrusted to professional hands and scandalmongers have their heyday, often leading to tragic outcomes: to the nation's detriment, the better traducer wins the day. Nevertheless, if the enormous amount of gossip and slander that are transacted daily and the energy invested in producing and responding to them are considered, the actual visible effect of tale-bearing appears small.

In dealing with any form of tale-bearing one has to determine its truth value. And when its content is not wholly fictitious, one must differentiate those elements which present particulars of reality and those which have been added by the tale-bearer. In most, but not all, instances, the product is a mixture of both. It would facilitate research in the psychology of detraction if it were possible to determine with certainty which parts of a detracting statement reproduce events and processes that have actually occurred. In general, this determination requires methods that lead outside psychology.

Jung (1910) initiated the psychoanalysis of gossip by contributing a charming observation. A 13-year-old girl was discharged from school for having spread a rumor alleging a male teacher's improper behavior toward her. It turned out that she had told two girl-friends a dream of seemingly harmless content in which the teacher played a major role. The rumor that her two confidantes set afloat contained many events that were derived from the dream's manifest content, but the lewd act toward the girl that was part of the rumor did not show up in the manifest dream. The remarkable feature of the incident was that the teacher's alleged improper behavior was the content of a correct interpretation of the *unconscious* meaning derived from the "harmless" dream facade. The rumor conveyed the girl's repressed sensuous, erotic wishes regarding the teacher. The teacher's improper action had never occurred in reality but was the content of an actually existing *psychic* reality. The rumor was untrue insofar as a derivative of a dream element was presented as having occurred in reality. As it turned out, reality had been bare of any impropriety, but the exploration of the rumor led to relevant psychological facts, namely, the girl's dream and its correct interpretation as revealed in the rumor. It is rather exceptional that the truth content of gossip can be clarified so neatly as happened in Jung's clinical investigation, but it is a striking example of an instance of gossip whose content did not reproduce an event of external reality but still contained a significant psychological truth.

Many years ago, when I began to be intrigued by the problem of gossip, I retrieved instances of gossip about myself in my home town, where it was not difficult to do, and thus was able to assay the truth value that may be contained in detraction. I was struck by the fact that, though lacking a basis in social reality, the slander was by no means independent of what went on in my unconscious. I was surprised by the rich strands connecting the content of the tale with repressed imagery, wishes, impulses and their like. Despite divergences between the malicious report and the repressed contents, the correspondence between some of their elements was sufficient to make their connection discernible. The misrepresentations appeared to be derivatives of contents lying dormant in their target. The factual truth value was zero, but the psychological truth value was considerable, this following the pattern of what Jung had found decades before.

Just as one distinguishes "good" and "bad" painters, one may distinguish "good" and "bad" gossipers. The good gossiper is the one who projects the right content into the right place, to all appearances divining his victim's unconscious; this does not preclude the operation in the gossiper of the psychopathology I have outlined earlier.

To illustrate another type of gossiper: I once retrieved a piece of talk about myself for which I was unable to find a referent. It had been originated by a person of the kind I call a "pathological slanderer." Her misstatements apparently contained nothing but derivatives of her own unconscious without reflecting anything that, to my best knowledge, could be attributed to me in any form, conscious or unconscious.

"Good" gossipers, to the contrary, are paranoid personalities with a particular flair for the archaic in their contemporaries. The kind of gossip for which no reality equivalent (factual or psychological) can be unearthed by any method of exploration—the product of a poor or "bad" gossiper—I shall call confabulation, for the time being. It is often colorful and attractive to the recipient; at the same time, it can provide insights—occasionally even deep ones—into the talebearer.[5]

IV

At this point I turn to my own clinical experience and present two examples of the contamination of transference by detraction that reached patients from the outside. In the course of their occurrence I was confronted with the specific technical problems provoked by the disparagement of the therapist and became familiar with the problems' general clinical aspect; in addition, the two experiences occasioned the study of their effect not only on patients but also on myself, which is included as a kind of psychological postmortem. Two authors (Gay, 1988; Young-Bruehl, 1988) have charged me with odious behavior, and their allegations came to the attention of some of my patients before they reached me. The explication of their charges that follows may be skipped by the reader interested primarily in ways of dealing with

[5]Whether gossip and slander find credence in the listener does not depend on their truth value. Confabulation often finds surprising belief. Successful transmission of a tale and its truth content are independent variables.

the psychoanalytic situation arising from such complications.

a

Peter Gay took me to task for the way he was certain I acted as secretary of the Sigmund Freud Archives, and in doing so he did not spare recourse to
offensive language. In the Acknowledgments at the
end of his Freud biography (Gay, 1988, pp. 781–786)
he introduced me with high praise, as having "earned
the gratitude of all scholars doing research on Freud
and the history of psychoanalysis," by virtue of pro-
moting the Archives' transactions. Yet this was followed by his oppugning general policies he claimed
I adhered to. "Dr. Eissler," he continued, "has freely
and frequently expressed the view that anything—I
mean *anything*—that Freud had not intended for publication should not be published" (Gay's emphasis;
p. 784). Gay would be embarrassed if he were pressed
to cite a single instance in which I said anything of
that sort. If the falsity of his statement needed any
proof, I could cite two pieces I published that Freud
had not intended for publication: a letter he wrote as
a late adolescent (Eissler, 1972) and five aphorisms
written at age fifteen for a school paper (Freud, 1871)
were edited by me.

I can as easily dispose of another serious charge of
his, which reads as follows: "The addiction to secrecy
to which Dr. Eissler was—and is—so passionately
committed could only encourage the festering of the
most outlandish rumors about the man whose reputation he was trying to protect. . . . I have been corresponding with Dr. Eissler on this vexed issue for almost twenty years now, and have been asking for

material he controls ever since the writing of this biography became a possibility. But the results have always been the same for me—total defeat" (Gay, 1988, p. 784f.). Gay is mistaken. It can be proved that he visited my office on a Sunday afternoon in 1984 and on that occasion asked for access to the correspondence of Freud with the Reverend Oscar Pfister (1873–1956). He was assured of the Archives' cooperation with his request to receive a copy of the correspondence, which disproves prima vista a passion for secrecy on my part. However, for reasons to be explained presently, I had to stipulate the reservation that he would accept the editorship of the letters, to which he agreed. But later he did not come to terms with the publisher. In any event, it is plain that his imputation of addiction to secrecy has no substance.

The reservation concerning editorship of the correspondence touches upon a subject for which not only I but the Archives have been severely castigated and which deserves clarification. At its inception in 1952, the Archives imposed restrictions on its holdings, in conformity with the intent and decision of its founders as well as Anna Freud's wishes. When Anna Freud withdrew her objections in the late 1970s, the way to the publication of Freud's letters was opened. The Archives welcomed the prospect but was determined to insist that only editions conforming to the highest scholarly standards should reach the reader. Glaring errors had abounded in many of the letters that had been published previously: they had been adulterated by misreadings of Freud's handwriting, serious mistakes in translation, and misinterpretations of sentences torn out of context. Never-sagging vigilance was to make sure that such literary felonies were not repeated. In order to protect the letters against disfigurements of that sort, the Archives, as long as I was its secretary, was firm in its resolve that the first step toward the publication of a series of letters—and the Archives planned to publish Freud's correspondence with each of various individuals—was the appointment of a conscientious editor of high standing. I was delighted when Gay—whom I at that time judged to be a trustworthy editor—consented to edit Freud's letters to a close collaborator that had been accessible only in an abridged, insufficiently annotated publication.

The reader may believe such precautionary measures to be exaggerated; I shall illustrate what may happen when authors rely on their own wits and go unchecked by experienced translators, editors and publishers. Freud used an elegant turn of phrase in a letter to Sandor Ferenczi (1873–1933) introducing Ernest Jones (1879–1958), who was to start his training analysis with Ferenczi: "Feed the chrysalis so that it can become a queen bee" (cf. Hoffer, 1989). In Young-Bruehl's biography of Anna Freud, this was transmogrified into "Put some stuffing in the clown, so we can make him a king" (Young-Bruehl, 1988, p. 62). Her knowledge of the German language aside, she should have realized that a vulgarity of the kind she thought to have discovered was beyond Freud.

It will be rightly asked why not more, if not all, Freud letters have been published. Until recently, the extraordinary expenses of transcribing and editing were nearly unsurmountable. Since the Freud Literary Heritage Foundation has begun to provide funds for these purposes, this hindrance has been reduced. One would expect that with the elimination of that limitation, the floodgates would open and an abundance of choice editions of Freud letters would reach the market. Nevertheless, scholarly editions of Freud letters are endangered because the present Board of the Archives insists on a restriction that is contrary to custom and unacceptable to scholarly editors. The Board decided that copies of letters will be released to users only after the names of his patients have been made illegible. The Archives' precautionary measure is justified, with only one exception. It should not be applied to a scholar to whom the preparation of Freud letters for publication has been entrusted. Such an editor is carefully selected by a university, the Freud Copyrights, Inc., and a publisher. When, additionally, the manuscript is submitted to the Archives for approval before publication, no indiscretion can occur. A scholarly editor must be acquainted with a patient's identity, if this can be established at all, for the sake of clarifying the content. This is a fundamental obligation of an editor that cannot be abrogated. It is worth noticing that Gay himself is fully aware of the impropriety of revealing the names of Freud's patients and demands that scholars should sign "a rigorous statement . . . making each user promise not to publish . . . the identity of a patient [of Freud's]" (Gay, 1988, p. 785). Nevertheless, he infringed upon that principle in his biography without ostensible reason or necessity. This caused me great chagrin, for I had promised the patient's daughter that her mother's identity would never be revealed. One would have assumed, prior to Gay's offense, that no responsible editor would reveal the names of patients.

The ease with which editorships of Freud letters are mismanaged cannot be overrated. I shall not refrain from presenting another example, which I discovered when I accidentally came across the original of one of the letters Gay was privileged to publish for the first time in his biography. On October 6, 1910, Freud wrote a letter of major importance to Ferenczi, of which Gay offers the reader only a few sentences, torn out of context. Freud was at that time engaged in a formidably thorny and delicate venture. Before him lay the printed pages of the most detailed record ever written by a highly educated, sensitive man who had been devastated, at least temporarily, by a grave mental disorder and who tried with a gigantic effort to find a way through the frightening perplexities of the protean excrescences his mind gave birth to. Virgil's task, when leading Dante, was easier than Freud's taking on the challenge of leading his reader through that pandemonium. And yet, his staying power defied the seemingly unattainable. Freud was probing for the meaning of the famous *Memoirs of My Nervous Illness* (Schreber, 1903), the reminiscences of Daniel Paul Schreber (1842–1911), the president of a High Court in Saxony, who had fallen prey to a florid paranoid psychosis. It had become evident to Freud that the colorful, fantastic and mysterious autobiographical presentation, which at first reading leaves the impression of a galimatias, was meaningful when understood as being rooted in the patient's conflicts with his father. In his letter to Ferenczi Freud raised the question of the modality that may have been operative in that relationship.

Before indicating how Gay mangled the meaning of this passage, I wish to point out that the letter permits a glimpse of Freud's creative process. The way Freud used Schreber's language in his letter testifies to the internal echoing of Schreber's conflicts as well as the extent to which Freud threw himself into his subject's existence. That language grew out of primordial layers and was drenched in archaic feelings. Freud was immensely attracted by its idiosyncratic tempestuousness, and he used some of Schreber's typical expressions in a fitting and penetrating manner. Thus, one can observe how deeply Freud was immersed in the subject of his investigation and exploration—the language being the bridge over which he crawled into his subject's guts, possibly diminishing distance occasionally to almost identity.

In the same letter, in conformity with the document he was studying, he expatiated on the paternal role he himself held in his relationship with his collaborator, Ferenczi, and on his relationship to his three sons. Thus, even as he was deeply absorbed in the enigmas of Schreber's personality, Freud projected himself outside; he looked both at himself and at the subject of exploration in the process of carefully checking the meaning that the topic of research had for him personally.

It is the traces of that dimension which make the document so important. In it one stumbles upon a triangle that is formed, first, by the dizzy height of a challenging problem, second, by Freud's restless, ever-inquisitive mind longing and pushing for the conversion of the recondite into clear insight, and, third, by the observer watching himself while the wrestling between the first two goes on. The picture comes to mind of a superior mind evaluating an ongoing chess game between two masters.

The outcome was the demonstration that what had looked like nonsensical eruptions of a disturbed mind were manifestations of aspirations that were contradictory and in acute conflict and on the way toward establishing a form of psychopathology that was new in his life and amounted to something like a precarious equilibrium.

And what does Gay have to say? Nothing in Freud's letter gives cause for describing the significant question he asked Ferenczi about Schreber's father as "rhetorically, teasingly borrowing his language from Schreber" (Gay, 1988, p. 283). Freud's question was raised in deepest seriousness. Gay, even though he is not unaware of the importance of Freud's essay, is Boeotian enough to declare that Freud "derived much comic relief from Schreber," and that Freud and his collaborators used Schreber's vocabulary "gleefully" (p. 279). He reaches the level of the truly freakish when he mocks Freud as being "a little callous" in using "comical Schreberisms" (p. 280). What struck Gay as comical were attestations of the degree to which Freud penetrated into an exceptional personality that had the misfortune to be changed into an organization deprived of an essential, controlling function and therefore lost understanding empathy toward his contemporaries. Through Schreber's language Freud gained access to a territory that is firmly closed to minds like Gay's.

Yet Gay's misreading of Freud's letter is not the only defect; he made a mistake in his translation and put a plural where Freud had written a singular. I shall not belabor that error which, small as it seems, is grave inasmuch as it makes Freud appear in the undeserved light of overestimating the consequences of his essay.

In conclusion, it may be stated that as much as free access to documents would satisfy democratic expectations, such a ruling would favor the abuse of documents in the case of the Sigmund Freud Archives if instituted prior to scholarly publication of its holdings. It would lead to the imposition of misinformation on an unsuspecting and defenseless readership, bereft of the possibility of checking on the author's statements.

b

I had barely succeeded in helping my patients overcome the jolt Gay's critical comments delivered to their confidence when they had to face a new blow to their trust in me. In Elisabeth Young-Bruehl's aforementioned biography of Anna Freud, the reader learns that in 1971, when Anna Freud after an absence of 33 years returned to Vienna for a week on the occasion of the 27th Congress of the International Psychoanalytic Association, she

> brought both her grief and her whimsy with her. She escaped the hour-by-hour schedule Kurt Eissler had prepared for her in his self-appointed role as her manager—a role she did not want him to assume but which she could not bring herself to refuse him—and went to the museum . . . [Young-Bruehl, 1988, p. 402].

Here is an instance of the detractor's self-betrayal of unreliability to which I referred earlier, for in the same breath, Young-Bruehl acknowledges Anna Freud's leading role at the Congress. This obviously meant that the short period of her stay in Vienna was overcrowded with professional appointments that had been scheduled prior to her arrival and therefore were beyond my power to arrange. Outside of these obligations, as Young-Bruehl reports, Anna Freud participated in a private performance, arranged especially for her at Vienna's famous Spanish Riding School, and attended a meeting at the Austrian Ministry of Education; she visited with her father's B'nai B'rith lodge, where she gave a lecture, and met with old schoolmates as well as with European and American émigré friends (p. 403). Young-Bruehl cannot have been so naïve as to assume that I could have had a hand in the arrangement of these multifarious events. Therefore, she is as much to blame for her detraction as those who misinformed her.

Some of Anna Freud's activities remained unrecorded. When she visited her beloved former country estate, Hochroterd, for an afternoon, I accompanied her. At the villa of Dr. Solms, the president of the Vienna Psychoanalytic Society, she participated in a meeting of Congress officers, from which I was absent. Contrary to Young-Bruehl, she attended a reception at the City Hall.

The reader will rightly ask how it happens that I am so well informed about Anna Freud's whereabouts during her stay. When I arrived in Vienna, I was asked by Dr. Solms to function as her escort, a request I had no reason to refuse. I was supposed to assure transportation and protect her from journalists and photographers, toward whom, as Young-Bruehl knows, Anna Freud felt an intense aversion. Of course she was informed of my assignment and seemed to have no objection. I was told by her from day to day where and when I should wait for her. The idea that she would have hesitated to tell me when she was in no need of an escort has no validity. Besides, anyone who had even an inkling of her personality would know that she would never put up with a person as intrusive and supercilious as I appear to be in Young-Bruehl's description.[6]

V

As I noted, Gay as well as Young-Bruehl are confabulators; their detractions do not reveal anything of either an external or an internal reality. To have imposed a schedule on Anna Freud would have been alien and objectionable to me. It is an action that would have been discordant with my temperament.

I was in doubt for some time whether I should call Gay's detraction a confabulation when he rebuked me for an alleged aversion toward the publication of Freud letters. However, my doubt was allayed when I found a quotation in Young-Bruehl's book (1988, p. 438) from a letter that Anna Freud had written me after the publication of the Fliess letters, in which she asked that I "see to it that . . . publication of the Freud correspondences would stop for a number of

[6] I am persona non grata for Young-Bruehl. Of her many critical remarks about me, I want to discuss only one more. She implies that I "seal" the Archives (Young-Bruehl, 1988, p. 433) in order to hide secrets, but ignores my lack of knowledge of the contents of the Archives' holdings, almost all of which were deposited in the Library of Congress without my having read them; she also ignores my attempts to organize the publication of Freud's letters.

years." I found no trace of this demand in my memory—it was evidently forgotten. If Gay had been right, at least with respect to unconscious desires or tendencies, I am forced to conclude that I would have pounced upon her request as a welcome excuse for opposing further publication, whereas my policy was the opposite. My forgetting Anna Freud's wish strongly suggests that Gay, too, is a confabulatory detractor.

Thus Gay and Young-Bruehl have in common that their misrepresentations are confabulations, but in another respect there is a difference. In Young-Bruehl's instance it is obscure why she goes out of her way to belittle me. In contrast, I have an idea as to why Gay berated me. A misrepresentation of his that I have not yet mentioned was suggestive. Gay alerts his readers "to gaps in this biography for which I am not responsible, gaps I tried in vain to close" (Gay, 1988, p. 784), the worst of which, he claims, was the one I caused by denying him access to "the collection of letters that Freud and his fiancée exchanged during the five long years of their engagement" (p. 785). Gay holds me, whom Anna Freud had designated as a custodian of those letters, the famous *Brautbriefe*, responsible for his inability to have access to them. This is an exercise in guile, for he had been informed by two sources that Anna Freud had restricted that correspondence to the year 2000.

With regard to Gay's excuse, one may ask: why would an author feel obliged to apologize at all for a condition caused by the unavailability of documentation, particularly when, as Prof. Gerhard Fichtner's private concordance indicates, 284 letters have been published, in full or in part, covering the four and a quarter years of Freud's engagement? Few other periods in Freud's life are equally well documented, as a perusal of Gay's own publication will readily confirm. Gay's uncalled-for self-defense, which led to an uncalled-for accusation, covers up a self-reproach. His pretense of a gap made me a handy scapegoat for the many deficiencies of his biography.

The auspices for a good biography were not favorable when entrusted to his hands, for Gay did just that against which Leonardo da Vinci warned the painters of portraits—he projected himself into the subject whose biography he was composing. The outcome was not much more than the history of a person of talent, a Horatio Alger-type success story about a Jewish boy of low station who by happenstance was thrown into a big city and there made remarkable discoveries, but was otherwise a usually ill-tempered, rather cantankerous, authoritarian non-believer, who erred surprisingly often during his career. Only on page 639, from Leonard Woolf's mouth, does the reader hear a pronouncement for which he has not been prepared, namely, that Freud "was not only a genius, but also, unlike many geniuses, an extraordinarily nice man. . . . [He] had an aura, not of fame, but of greatness." This statement is all the more impressive since it comes from a man who found the famous people of his time, most of whom he knew, "disappointing or bores, or both" (Woolf, 1967, as quoted by Gay, 1988, p. 639). Through the fortuitous transmission of Woolf's observation, the reader finally learns who Freud really was.

There are other defects. Gay fails to discern the nodal importance of a childhood experience, which he does not even mention. Freud's mother demon-strated to the incredulous boy *ad oculos* the inescapa-bility of death: she simply rubbed the palms of her hands together and showed him the resulting black-ish scales of epidermis, thereby proving that man is made of dust (Freud, 1900, pp. 204–208). The little boy could hardly believe his eyes. In that moment, the foundation was laid for what might almost be called an addiction of Freud's to demonstrate *ad oculos*, over and over again, that what may to the average mind be most improbable was truth. Like-wise, Gay overlooked Freud's identification with Hamlet and Macbeth, the latter already detectable in an early letter (Freud, 1960, p. 6). Nowhere is there an intimation in Gay's book that Freud's writings are, as Goethe said of his own opus, "fragments of a great confession," or that they had changed the climate of the Western world.

Nevertheless, his biography has been successful. This should not give occasion for surprise, for a book that contains so many quotations from Freud letters as Gay's does cannot but leave the reader deeply touched. Gay was given the privilege of using Freud's correspondence with Ferenczi, Jones and others. It stands to reason that if Gay could have laid his hands on those *Brautbriefe* which have not yet been pub-lished, they would have elicited no less enthusiasm then those already published, and the reader would have been dazzled all the more. When Gay read his manuscript it may have dawned on him that his text fell flat and could not rival the letters in sparkle; the limpness of his own contribution might well have frightened him, and the shift to rage at me could then have given him relief.

But I must admit that it may turn out that I will have to apologize to Gay. Have I not done him an injustice by taking seriously what he intended to be nothing but a joke? He has, after all, become quite famous as a jester. Years ago he purported to have discovered a surprisingly early review of Freud's *Interpretation of Dreams* in an obscure Austrian journal, a translation of which he duly published. Recently it was established that there was no such journal and that the review was a complete fabrication. Gay had ample reasons to laugh heartily at the simplicity and naïveté of those who had accepted its authenticity. It was all great fun for him.

Likewise, on even better grounds, he may laugh at those who take the Acknowledgments concluding his Freud biography and containing his animadversions in earnest. He will ask, and rightly so, how anybody could suppose even for a moment that a man of his intelligence and maturity could be so vain as to introduce himself to the reader by comparing himself in all seriousness to Whistler (Gay, 1988, p. 781). He will expect, and reasonably so, that readers will understand that only a comic motive would compel him to enumerate twenty of his lectures and to congratulate himself on providing so many "stimulating and invaluable" occasions (p. 782). No one, he will argue, could be so dull-witted as not to see that all of this is delicious satire in the service of establishing a new form of parody: the Self-Acknowledgment.

Similarly, when, toward the end of his Acknowledgments (p. 785) Gay laments all the epistolary treasures that were denied him, he will rest assured that readers will catch his drift. Who among them will be able to resist asking whether it was ever the case that an author recorded in his Acknowledgments that which he did *not* get and those that did *not* give? Who could be so dense as not to detect his impish intent in making the Acknowledgments an occasion for twitting the ungracious? Could any but the most hapless reader fail to conclude that Gay had invented yet another mock genre: the Dis-Acknowledgment?

When all is said and done, one must admit that Gay is very good at hoaxes. Regrettably, on the way from hard to soft cover, he seems to have lost some of his zest for comedy, for while he preserved the Self-Acknowledgment, he dropped the Dis-Acknowledgment.

As difficult as it is to believe, many people do not get Gay's jokes. Evidently there is a "gap" between his sense of humor and that of the common man. If he wishes to keep amusing readers everywhere with his literary pranks, I should advise him invariably to let them know when they are supposed to laugh and when to cry.

VI

Gay's and Young-Bruehl's accusations refer to more or less unimportant matters; however, that does not diminish their suitability as subjects for a discussion of an appropriate analytic technique of handling unwelcome incidents of that kind. I was apprised of Young-Bruehl's detraction by an older lady who had been in psychoanalytic face-to-face therapy for many years. Her positive transference was, I am certain, jolted by what she read about me. She was vague in her report of embarrassing references to my imposing

myself on Anna Freud in Vienna. I was certain she
was mistaken and replied that I would check. It took
me a long time to get hold of the book, and in the
meantime she touched on her uneasiness about my
alleged obtrusiveness only once or twice. Whether
she believed the detraction was not clear; she seemed
to have forgotten the whole incident by the time I
had found out what Young-Bruehl had claimed; there
the matter came to rest, without diminishing the patient's strong, positive transference. Another patient,
who was in analysis, responded in a lively way, em-
phasizing her conviction that I could never have acted
so boorishly; the story must be a big lie. She never
again referred to it.

It happens occasionally that patients find a conve-
nient way out when they face the dilemma of having
to verbalize negative insinuations about the therapist.
A male patient whose suspicion was easily aroused
had gone through several long-lasting, most painful
bouts in which he had lost all confidence in me.
Young-Bruehl's presentation could not have left a
doubt about my utterly ill-mannered way of dealing
with Anna Freud, and therefore would very likely
have precipitated a new spell of distrust. However,
he avoided the resurgence of agonizing doubts by
treating her tale the way a dreamer sometimes treats
an unpleasant day residue: he turned it into its opposite. He expressed his admiration for how superbly I
organized Anna Freud's time when she was in New
York. He exchanged New York for Vienna and at the
same time reversed grating criticism into commenda-
tion. His hypersensitivity to aggressive feelings
brought about a strong resistance to the perception
of reality as it was, which saved me by a hairsbreadth

from losing him as a patient. A distortion of reality of that kind usually undermines a patient's secure hold on reality; in this instance, however, it served to make it possible for the patient to eschew a grave conflict threatening a questionable outcome.

Gossip may sometimes not appear to be injurious and destructive, namely, when it effects an increase in positive transference. An analysand recalled having heard that once I was in danger of being shot by an intruder armed with a rifle, but that in the course of a drawn-out session lasting several hours I quieted him down. I was baffled because nothing of its kind had ever happened to me. However, it dawned on me after a while that the story in all likelihood referred to an incident of over 20 years ago, when an out-of-state colleague called me in an emergency. A patient of his, a famous actor who was passing through New York, had just informed him of his intention to commit suicide.

I came face to face with a man, staying alone in a hotel room, who no doubt was in acute distress but resolved to keep silence about his anguish. He refused hospitalization, nor could I persuade him to take a sedative. It was evident that under these circumstances the only honorable retreat I could beat was to insist that he hand me the two rifles I had noticed. When he found out that this was the only way to get rid of me, he complied. I never heard of him again. How that story could have survived even in its distorted form was puzzling. I am certain I had mentioned it rarely, and this merely because of the episode's amusing consequence—the disturbing problem of getting two rifles into my building without this being noticed by the doorman or a tenant. This rumor, too, carries the earmark of conversion into the opposite: the danger of the patient's suicide into the danger of a murderous assault. The patient who brought it up in the treatment called my action a heroic deed. Yet tales of that kind are in their own way also injurious to the course of treatment. Myths of unusual qualifications or exploits, when prompted by external sources, become incrustations on the transference that are often immune to dissolution because they appear to be assured as facts and therefore defy analysis.

As in real life, so also in the therapeutic situation: the truth value of rumors and gossip and the probability of their reception by patients are two independent variables: a rumor that conveys what really happened may be disbelieved, and an outlandish one readily accepted. Even though Gay's animadversions were unfounded, he was successful in inducing readers to believe them. Most of my patients responded in the same way and took exception to my narrowness and rigidity and the obstacle they created to the free growth of biographical research on Freud. They were certain that I feared lest some letters compromise Freud—evidently I had to hide documents in order to preserve the ideal image that Jones had allegedly created in his Freud biography. One patient encouraged me to have confidence in Freud's greatness and lift all restrictions.

Depending on circumstances, a difficult situation may arise when an analyst is unaware of the existence of a rumor and gossip about him. Once, Muriel Gardiner called me to apologize for a devastating statement about me in a widely read magazine, which a derelict journalist had attributed to her but which she had never made. The incident had not come to my attention, and it struck me that none of my patients had made mention of it. Under such circumstances, one faces a technical dilemma. Should one ask a patient whose resistance seems intractable whether something unfavorable about the therapist has come to his attention? Patients do not like to bring such information out into the open. I have observed that, paradoxically enough, for many patients it is easier to broach their irrational transference imagery than it is to mention an actually existing defect they have discerned in the therapist. It is as if they were somehow aware of the irrationality of the distortions brought about by transference and rightly anticipated that the analysis will restore the former untainted image, whereas the perception of a real defect threatens to disfigure the therapist's image irreparably. Rather than expose themselves to that painful possibility, they deny knowledge of the real defect and keep it unverbalized. When gossip containing a negative reference reaches them, they are prone to believe that there must or may be some truth in the matter. The threat of the ensuing diminution of positive feelings causes patients to keep secret from the therapist their awareness of his unwelcome and objectionable depiction, which they fear may be based on reality.

At the time of Dr. Gardiner's call, I had to wrestle with an exceptional, intractable resistance in a patient. In vain had I approached his negative responses as part of his transference; the information I had received, however, opened the possibility that they were based on his reaction to the defamatory statement. If the patient's resistance was a bona fide transference reaction, my asking him for an outside source would precipitate unnecessary questions, mislead him and cause ripples in the psychoanalytic process. In this instance, good luck was on my side. He readily admitted that he tried to circumvent a discussion of what he had read. The resistance was inactivated and the way was open to investigate his difficulty in tolerating an image of the therapist that was imperfect.

It will be objected that I exaggerate the dilemma. It is true that there are no earmarks that would signal the origin of a long-lasting resistance, that is, whether it derives from internal causes or is prompted by information from outside. However, in analyzing a resistance provoked by external stimulation, one discovers in the same process internal sources: the two are not isolated but intimately intertwined. Yet although this is undeniably true, there is the danger that the external source is not brought to light at all. It would weaken the momentum of the analytical process if inner motives, valid as ever they may be, were pursued while the patient is struggling with complications rooted in external reality that escape verbalization. The only way out would be to rely on one's intuition, which is often misleading unless one is privileged by the possession of unusual talents.

In one instance when I interfered with the patient's associations, I was less fortunate. His analysis was made difficult by a precariously shaky transference. He began to read Gay's biography shortly before the start of the summer vacation that would interrupt treatment for a long time. He wondered why my name did not show up in the index. I felt certain that he would reach the incriminating remarks, which are at the end of the book, during the recess. To anticipate the strong reaction that might occur in my absence, I told him that he would come across my name in further reading. When he came to the next session, he was furious about my stupidity in opposing Gay's access to the Archives' holdings and expressed annoyance over my encouraging him to look for my name. Had I not interfered, he would not have checked the Acknowledgments and would have been spared a few distasteful moments. The patient's objection was not without merit, I thought.

VII

These are a few superficial clinical situations, selected at random, that may result when the analyst is denigrated in a way that reaches patients. Is there a specific psychoanalytic method or technique to counteract complications brought about on such occasions? The technique dictated by psychoanalytic common sense seems straightforward and does not leave alternatives to the initial steps to be taken. One has to explore the patient's imagery about the entire issue—to which part of the aspersion he attributes reality and to which part, invention. Insight into the motivation of what induces him to choose either is indispensable. As noted before, some patients do not reveal these details easily. One will receive a variety of responses depending on the phase of transference and contingent circumstances. A patient made the slander of the therapist the carrier of inimical feelings he had suppressed until then, and felt triumphant that he now shared a secret, in the form of the denigration, which he was not supposed to know and which had leaked out at last. He had been exceedingly curious and raised many a question about the

analyst that had remained unanswered. The knowledge that he received at last was welcomed as a compensation for the uncertainty he had to endure when
the analyst kept silence in response to his many questions.

A detraction may interfere with the minimum of
idealization that will keep a treatment on an even
keel; it can even cause a tear in the therapeutic relationship from which the patient will not recover easily. It may become the core of a depression.

In most of this, the repetition of early experiences
is detectable. I surmise that the traumatic, sudden
depreciation of an idealized analyst may prompt a
regression to an early phase of infancy when the patient was traumatized by separation. However,
knowledge of the therapist's denigration does not always result in a damaged relationship to the therapist. Under exceptional conditions it may accelerate
the analytic process. Under the impact of the knowledge gained the patient may become aware of his
overestimation and dependency and be spurred on
to activity that otherwise would have been delayed.

It goes without saying that the subject matter concerns an infinite variety of combinations depending
on type and content of deprecation, state of transference and phase of treatment at the time when the
patient is apprised of the derogation and, on the other
hand, the specific nature of the patient's childhood
traumata. Each instance, it will be contended, requires its own solution, which shuts out rules and
precludes the groping for a standard technique. But
does a satisfactory technique exist? There is one feature that is attached to each instance of derogation
and provides a singular angle that is not encountered

in other clinical predicaments. I refer to the effect of slander on the therapist himself. The saying *semper aliquid haeret* has an ancient provenance. It refers to the social image of the slandered person that, as the sentence insists, will always suffer some permanent disfiguration. The *semper aliquid haeret* may be turned around and be understood psychologically as the change that slander effects, not in the slandered person's social image but in the slandered person's image of himself, in his identity. What are the effects of detraction on the maligned therapist? on his relationship to the patient?

Evidently the maligned therapist's inner response must be taken under advisement before the question of the appropriate psychoanalytic technique can be tackled at all. A slurred person's reaction will vary with the kind of slur encountered. If it is of a preposterous nature it will be ineffective and easily dismissed. But when the maligned person's social image is in danger of being altered, or is actually altered, the victim has no reliable channel for rectifying the falsification. The uncertainty about the degree of modification his image has suffered in the eyes of the social group may leave a lesion in his self-image. As is known, if the self-image is firmly established, it may prove invulnerable, even under incredible stresses. A Jewish child learning from early on that he belongs to a group chosen by God among all other nations had a chance, as an adult, of going through the execrable torments and humiliations of the concentration camp without diminution of self-respect. Even when severe and permanent neuroticism was caused by enormous traumatization, the feeling of identity may have survived uninjured, as long as the early teaching of being chosen has not been destroyed. The torturer's assault recoiled upon himself; his brutality proved all the more his inferiority. The true believer left the camp with the same conviction of being chosen with which he had entered it. Many Jews wore the Yellow Star with pride.

An identity that is set up on such solid ground, however, may weaken in its self-assessment and suffer injury from even relatively slight abuse when the assault cannot be made to recoil on the attacker because he is a member of the community. Then the detractor may make the maligned person's community accept as true to fact the image altered by slander or libel and this may impinge on the victim's feeling of identity. It cannot be determined what a "normal" response would be to a detraction that has become part of a permanent record. Though the victim cannot remove the actual injury that his public image has suffered, he may through defensive responses try to counteract a permanent subjective injury, and actually succeed in this effort. But it may just as well happen that the objective disfigurement will leave a trace in the self-image. One encounters here the operation of a mechanism that is the reverse of the mechanism observed in paranoid psychoses. In that group of disorders the patient projects onto the outer world an inner process that results in the formation of a delusion about the outer world. However, when the denigrator reaches his goal and the community accepts his limning of the target as correct, society then has formed an erroneous image that it persistently projects into the victim. If the denigrated person finally gives in to the pressure to which he is exposed, he is in danger of forming a "delusion" about his self, even when he is intellectually aware of its falseness. The defamed person struggles in vain to shake off the permanent effects that aggression penetrating from the outside in the form of the *aliquid haeret* has deposited in his image of self.[7]

Even if the maligned therapist escapes that danger and succeeds in working through the conflict aroused by the abuse and finds, for the time being, an unneurotic solution, the conflict may be reawakened and the equilibrium temporarily disturbed when, in the live and acute psychoanalytic treatment situation, the defamatory content appears in the patient's associations as if it were true to fact. Under such circumstances, the maligned therapist is confronted with a conflict that cannot be eliminated by self-analysis, for it is not a neurotic conflict but is, on analogy to reality anxiety, a reality conflict, which holds a unique position.

In the vast panorama of transference statements an analyst meets, it is taken for granted that the analyst's position and state of mind are exclusively concerned with the rule of *tua res agitur:* the patient's cause is transacted. That is, whatever a patient's specific transference reaction may mean to a therapist, the dyadic situation centers exclusively on the patient and his world. When, however, the animadversion to which the maligned therapist has been exposed makes its appearance in the patient's associations, the basic *tua res agitur* of the psychoanalytic dyad has been transformed for a moment into *mea res agitur:* that is, a part of the analyst's own world which is not

[7]As noted, there are some who are immune and not fazed by responses from their own community.

primarily and exclusively connected with that of the patient has entered the psychoanalytic transaction and become the point at issue. It is no longer the patient's world the therapist is facing but his own. The *tua res*, which belongs exclusively to the patient's world, moves for a while out of the therapist's focus. This must not be looked at as the unavoidable, so to speak legitimate, contamination of transference as a consequence of the analyst's appearance and habitat that I described initially. The detraction is a foreign body in the therapist's existence which stems from an external source, a social process he rejects, and which the analysand is misled into assessing as being located in the therapist. Understandably, this becomes the carrier of a personal reality conflict in the analyst.

VIII

My own reaction to Gay's and Young-Bruehl's aspersions surprised me. I had prided myself— wrongly, as it turned out—on being immune to the damaging imputations of others about me. This belief in my own immunity had come about after a friend and colleague had filed a complaint in court against me, charging that I had used undue influence on a patient whom he had sent into treatment with me. She was a relative of his and made me the heir of a substantial sum of money while she was on her deathbed (Eissler, 1955). The time it took until I was cleared of that suspicion was filled with anguish. When life resumed its normal course, I resolved never again to permit unconscionable intruders to carry unrest into my existence, and therefore I would never again take seriously what others said about me, as long as my own conscience was untroubled. I owe to Gay and Young-Bruehl the realization that my resolution was illusory. To be sure, what Gay or Young-Bruehl might have said about me meant nothing to me, but as soon as it became part of a printed record that found credence by virtue of the defamers' reputation, a feeling of helplessness and anger, combined with a subtle change of identity, took hold. Of course, my untoward response to their allegations was not nearly as severe as my response to my erstwhile friend's accusation had been. In that instance, the idea had seemed intolerable to me that somewhere there existed a court record that contained a sworn statement by a reputable physician that I had grossly violated professional standards and tried to misappropriate assets of a dying patient who was entrusted to my care. However, although I smarted under my colleague's charge, I was never exposed to the rudely interrupted continuum of the analyst's standard attitude by a switch from *tua* to *mea res agitur*, for the matter did not become known to any patient of mine and therefore never intruded upon the psychoanalytic situation. To be sure, what Gay and Young-Bruehl had to say about me were pinpricks when compared with my colleague's deposition in court. But their allegations were broached by patients and affected me in a strident way while analyzing. Thus, it happened that I failed in reaching a secure and satisfactory position regarding their charges.

The effect of unproven malicious assertions depends in part on the skill with which they are presented. Gay and Young-Bruehl did a good job in that respect. I infer this from the fact that none of my friends and acquaintances ever mentioned them. The allegations were accepted by them as correct: otherwise they would have expressed indignation at the abuse. Evidently Gay and Young-Bruehl convinced even those whose disposition toward me was friendly that there was some truth in their tales.

Slurs may become ineffective by reason of their absurdity, as I pointed out above. Esther Menaker (1989, p. 68) published a remark she claims I made to her 60 years ago when we became acquainted during her stay in Vienna. Austria's economic situation at that time was a disaster beyond words for all classes except the wealthy, and she was deeply moved by the utter misery, which was unimaginable for an American citizen. She is certain that I was "baffled" by her social concerns and even said, "But people are unemployed because they do not *want* to work" (Menaker's emphasis). Of the millions of sentences he has uttered during his lifetime, an adult recalls only a fraction. But at the same time he can be certain that an even larger number of sentences never crossed his mind, let alone his mouth. To give but an arbitrary example, I am absolutely sure that I never said, or thought—prior to the moment of searching for an example—that the U.S. Government should pay every Eskimo 25,000 dollars. Likewise, I am certain beyond a doubt that I never made a statement of the kind Menaker attributes to me.

Having grown up in an affluent surrounding, I was burdened from childhood on by a feeling of guilt. I was, and still am, unable to reconcile myself to the shameful injustice of unequal distribution of wealth.

Therefore, understandably, and as would have be-
fitted a Jewish student at that time anyhow, I joined
a left-of-center movement. The mere allusion to the
idea that the economic despair of Vienna could have
been self-willed by its victims would have made me
and my like-minded friends "see red." I am convinced that Esther Menaker confused me with someone else—all the more so as she never had brought
up that bizarre statement during decades of friendship. The patient who called my attention to Menaker's recollection rejected it as implausible. Whether
others responded to her censure in the same way I
do not know because I have not met another reader
of her book.

Gay and Young-Bruehl would never have been as
maladroit as Menaker. It is instructive to take cognizance of their technique. Both maximized *semper aliquid haeret* by following the added advice of *calumniare
audacter*, that is, if you want to be successful, calumni-
ate with audacity. This, indeed, they did and thereby
achieved the desired verisimilitude. Gay did not
merely state that I had once made the remark that
anything Freud did not want to have published
should not be published: he maintained that I expressed this belief "freely and frequently" (Gay, 1988,
p. 784), even putting "anything" in italics to make
sure that nobody could doubt the truthfulness of the
charge. Young-Bruehl not only claimed that I imposed my will on Anna Freud on this or that occasion—no, I had prepared "an hour-by-hour schedule" and got so much on her nerves that she had to
take flight from me into a museum. I could cite some
other remarks by Young-Bruehl in which she inti-
mates that Anna Freud could not trust me (e.g.,

Young-Bruehl, 1988, p. 411), but apparently the *audacter* was not strong enough in these instances, for no patient commented on them and therefore I leave them undiscussed in this publication. Young-Bruehl may pretend that distortions and untruths are the responsibility of her informants. She maintains having made a special effort to safeguard the truth by using statements only when "corroborated by at least one other interviewee" (p. 12). If truth were obtainable that simply and cheaply, even minds of limited or minor capacity would be in a position to write good biographies. Young-Bruehl will have to learn that two people with honest faces may be liars, while one whose countenance she does not like may speak the truth. A psychologically sophisticated biographer would, in assessing an informant's report, apply, among others, the criterion of *cui bono:* what are the informant's motives? was the informant jealous, frustrated, secretly angry at Anna Freud or someone close to her? did he have to repair a narcissistic injury? Aside from her reliance on counting noses, no precautionary measures in assessing the informant's reliability are found in Young-Bruehl's study.

In addition she infringes on academic standards, for she gives only a list of those she interviewed (p. 13f.) without identifying the specific source of each item of information she reproduced. Her omission of identifying witnesses lowers parts of her book to the level of a gossip column and gives rise to doubt in the credibility of some of her quotations. In the instance discussed she did not even notice that the detraction must be false, if for no other reason than that the circumstances she alleged were incompatible with each other.

IX

It now behooves me to point to some specific technical complications met in conjunction with the denigration of the analyst. When the meaning that the patient ascribes to the detraction, its strands to his past history, as well as the unconscious implications and the effects on the transference have been uncovered, has the psychoanalytic intervention ended optimally? Or is the patient entitled to know whether the negative statements that were brought to his attention were correct or incorrect, or to what extent they may have harbored a truth? Some analysts will deny the necessity of revealing anything of that kind to the patient. They may advise continuing the treatment undisturbed by whatever the patient may have heard about the therapist and believe to be true or not to be true.

I gratefully record Dr. Paul Parin's short communication that contravenes my views. Throughout the years of his analytic practice in Zurich wild rumors were bruited about him. However, this did not produce any difficulties in the treatment. He did not respond to these reports in any special way during the treatment, a strategy which did not disturb the analytic process. He observed that some patients believed, and at the same time disbelieved, the rumors, an observation that I, too, have made.[8]

[8]The oscillation between belief and disbelief finds a counterpart in the perceptive world. It is reminiscent of the oscillation in the perceptual reversal observed when viewing pictures in which figure/ground relationships are reversible.

Dr. Parin's experience was perhaps exceptional insofar as malicious rumors surrounded him from the beginning of his stay in Zurich. His social image was tainted from the outset by detractions. The patients seeking his treatment knew him from the inception of their acquaintance as a person whose social image was suspected by part of the community. Possibly, the technical problem under discussion is more likely to arise when the therapist's social image is conspicuously changed during the treatment. My guess would be that analysts in general would favor the idea or even assert emphatically that deprecation of the analyst does not require the institution of a special technique.

This would amount to the conclusion that whatever disreputable actions are attributed to the therapist, from whatever source, in the long run such accusations have to be taken by the patient as if they were empty prattle. All that the patient can rightfully expect from his therapist is the provision of treatment that lives up to optimal standards; the patient would under no circumstances be entitled to expect that the analyst furnish information about himself. I cannot accept that stance as fair. The patient's relationship with the therapist is kept buoyant by a font of good feelings. This font operates during phases of resistance and negative transference like a supply of capital that tides the economy over a recession. It may become invisible in the treatment but it is operative most of the time. If the reservoir were abolished or exhausted below a threshold level, the patient's confidence would vanish and the treatment would have to be terminated. A sinking below this minimum is forestalled and an impaired confidence restored when the negative transference is inactivated by interpretation, which makes it evident to the patient that his negative images and feelings had been the upshot of his own conflicts and not founded in external reality.

However, when negative inclusions in the patient's image of the therapist have been brought about by denigration of the therapist, the equilibrium will not necessarily be restored by interpretation alone. To be sure, some patients will deny the possibility that what they have heard about their analysts could be true. They develop a blind spot for the existence, or possible existence, of defects in their therapists and declare boldly that whatever the tales about their analysts are, they cannot be true. To be consistent, one has to show the patient that this conclusion is the effect of a positive transference, just as it is the effect of a negative transference when a patient believes malicious tales. In view of the patient's lack of realistic knowledge about the therapist, he is in no position to make a reliable assay about the truth or untruth of tales he may pick up. To repeat, the specific difficulty in the analysis of the patient's response to his therapist's denigration results from the transference nature of that response, positive or negative. It is always the upshot of transference and never based on the patient's trustworthy evaluation or on insight, since the patient is ignorant of his therapist's true personality. Unless it is of a preposterous nature, the possibility of the slander's truth remains unaffected by interpretation.

Of the many clinical possibilities, let me suggest a case of a patient who has heard the rumor that his analyst is an alcoholic or a drug addict or a homosexual. As far as I know, it has not yet been determined what type and degree of a therapist's psychopathology are compatible with his practicing psychoanalysis. It might not be out of the question that alcoholism is incompatible with optimal psychotherapeutic functioning. Would a patient not be entitled to know whether rumors of that kind do or do not contain truth? Recently, I was told an analyst who professed to be a homosexual proposed that only a manifest homosexual analyst is able to understand and analyze homosexual patients. This arrogation, besides illustrating the narcissistic overevaluation of self by some homosexuals, is basically wrong. But if the proposal were correct, a homosexual patient would have a right to know his analyst's sexual preferences.

One is reminded of Plato's idea that in order to be a good physician a person must have had diseases. This is partially true of analysts, for a person who never suffered from a neurosis, if this is feasible, would have no chance of becoming an adequate analyst. True as this is, however, it does not result in an obligation for the analyst to inform his patients as to his past psychopathology.

To return to the suspicions that could have been raised in my own case: would the patients have been entitled to know whether Gay's and Young-Bruehl's animadversions were correct? The behavior patterns for which I was blamed by them are not grossly offensive in themselves, but offensive enough to raise doubts about the therapist's suitability as a person capable of empathy and tact. A patient may dismiss Menaker's charge because of its bizarreness, but would he have reason to do the same regarding the other derogatory statements? If I had used undue influence on my colleague's relative, patients who had learned of it would have been right to withdraw their confidence. Similarly, if Gay and Young-Bruehl had been right, a patient cannot dismiss the possibility that I am boorish, lacking in manners, rigidly ruthless to deserving scholars, opinionated and biased. This may suffice to make him question, on seemingly objective grounds, my qualifications as a reliable, or at least tactful, analyst.

Depending on the circumstances, to convey to a patient the true background of a slander may become quite involved. A clarifying discussion about the suspicion of undue influence to which I had been exposed would have become unmanageable. The situation was rather simple regarding Gay's and Young-Bruehl's incriminations, whose falsity would have been established with a sentence in each instance: I had to serve as Anna Freud's escort, and I offered Gay the editorship of Freud letters.[9] The force of such declarations is greatly weakened if the patient rejoins that the analyst has no other choice but to plead innocent. "Even if guilty, would the therapist ever admit it?" would be a well-taken objection by the patient, who would have no reason to be convinced of the analyst's honesty under such circumstances. This rejoinder highlights the essential difference between the exigencies of transference resistances and those that may arise in response to a detraction. In the analysis of transference resistances there is no place for such a repartee.

Thus, of the two alternatives—limit oneself to interpretation and let the matter rest in itself, hoping the

---

[9]I would be confronted with an unsolvable entanglement if by ill luck a patient should come across what J. Masson and P. Roazen have, as I was told, written about me recently.

patient will not respond to the misrepresentation after a due period of time had lapsed, or tell the truth and clarify the reality situation—neither is satisfactory. Still another possibility to be considered is to choose the legal channel. I could have sued both authors. The verdict, assumedly favorable, would come to the patients' attention eventually and restore their faith, albeit after long delays. However, for obvious reasons I would prefer to bear the patients' belief in my boorishness and narrowness of mind rather than expose myself to the tribulations of years of litigation. Judge Learned Hand's famous statement is unforgettable.[10]

Here the psychoanalytic technique may face a constraint. It may be that the maligned analyst cannot be provided with a technique fulfilling the basic requirements that the psychoanalytic technique is expected to live up to. Libel may produce a reality impediment to the classical treatment that cannot be removed by interpretation. It may further turn out that there are public functions one should not pursue if one wishes to have an undisturbed psychoanalytic practice. It may be said that I should have made up my mind years ago about what was more important to me: to initiate and be active on behalf of the Archives, or to be an analyst.

X

At the bottom of the many problems I have raised and left dangling there is an issue that I tried to hold

[10]"I must say that, as a litigant, I should dread a law suit beyond almost anything else short of sickness and of death."

back because I am without an answer. Suppose, by a fortunate combination of circumstances, the patient would have found out by himself or otherwise discovered without interference on my part that the allegations he has read or heard about me are untrue: he still may ask with some justification, "What is it that makes just you the target of calumny?" The underlying question is that of how a person's reputation comes about. In other words, is a person responsible not only for his actions but also for his reputation? One aspect of victimology as I understand it may suggest an answer—in many instances, it holds the victim responsible for the crime.[11] Gay's and Young-Bruehl's comments, together with my colleague's complaint that I used undue influence on his relative, might, from this standpoint, speak in favor of the possibility that my unconscious has the effect of provoking others to raise incriminating or derogatory allegations against me. But Young-Bruehl's story as well as Gay's, I repeat, are confabulations, corresponding to nothing in either external or internal reality. It is puzzling how I could have prompted their assaults.

Where would one have to look for the subjective sources of a person's reputation? Its invisible roots remain obscure. In general, one is inclined to correlate behavior and reputation and, indeed, a person's reprobate actions frequently lead to an equivalent

---

[11]Oddly enough, this view harbors an optimistic outlook. Criminals do not want to be treated and, in any case, no one knows how to treat and cure them; but potential victims will be only too happy to be cured of their propensity to be victimized, and therefore one may anticipate the day when there will be a crime-free world, because there will be no more people desirous of becoming the victims of crime.

poor standing in the opinion of others. Yet this corre-
lation is a simplification in view of the large number
of instances that do not confirm it. Within reason,
behavior and reputation are two independent variables: there are those who repeatedly indulge in opprobrious activities without arousing any open or covert vituperation; on the other hand, faultless
conduct may remain unrevealed and the one who
practices it may earn disrepute. That is of particular
psychological interest because it demonstrates that
there is a factor operating outside the behavioral area
that has a decisive bearing upon a person's acknowledged and covert standing. The psychoanalytic mode
of thinking, based on a huge mass of evidence, forces
one to look for that factor in a person's unconscious.
This compels me to yield to the necessity of reconsid-
ering the possibility—even though there is no evidence for it—that, after all, in Gay's and Young-
Bruehl's allegations I faced more of my unconscious
than I had been ready to acknowledge.[12] It stands to
reason that one is more aware of the vulgarity of one's
contemporaries than of the devious ways in which
one's own unconscious peregrinates.

Previous evidence and inferences to the contrary
notwithstanding, I have formed the conviction that
even in instances in which the content of a detraction
seems totally alien to the victim in all respects—that
is, no link with his objective behavior as well as subjective (psychic) reality can be discovered—the defamation is a derivative of the defamed person's most

---

[12]One may object and claim that in view of the unconscious' infinity, one can
never be certain that no evidence could be potentially discovered in the repressed part of the personality. But this would amount to a form of begging the
question.

deeply repressed. The derogation then would contain the return of the repressed, which has found no previous outlet whatsoever in the defamed victim's imagery, ideation, action, symptom, or other kinds of psychopathology. I am unable to verify this proposition by demonstrating the connecting links between the archaic, deeply repressed and its return from the outside in the form of slander; I can only suggest as a hypothesis that in all instances slander is a fusion of the psychopathology of the slanderer and the psychopathology of the slandered. It sounds far-fetched to propose that what looks like the phantasmagoria of a paranoid slanderer should nevertheless contain derivatives of the firmly repressed, clinically otherwise inactive, mute parts of the victim's unconscious. But it is not so out of the way to ponder the possibility that the slanderer, whatever his personal psychopathology, is intuitively drawn toward a site of vulnerability in his victim. May not just that which is most perilous to a person's cynosure of identity be a part of the most deeply repressed? No wonder that a person confronted with such content will either reject it as totally invalid or feel deeply pained and injured by it.

We have returned once more to identity. One may vary Nietzsche's statement and say: The slanderer says, "That is what you are." The slandered says, "No, I am not that," but an imperspicuous voice gives assent. According to this construction, man can elude the voice of his unconscious, but not the voice of the slanderer.

* * * * *

Another aspect of slander is not unrelated to the

foregoing and may be linked to a historical development which a few analysts are certain has taken place; usually it is described in less radical terms than those I shall employ here. In its first two and one-half decades psychoanalysis stood under the sign of physical drives urgently striving for gratification. Of course, Freud was aware of the forces that softened the full brunt of wild physical unconscious imperatives, but the master who staged the show was the inexhaustible drive, the ego playing a subordinate role. How little Freud thought of it even in 1911 was intimated in a letter of 3 March to his confidant Jung, in which he wrote about Alfred Adler (1870–1937): "I never expected a psychoanalyst to be taken in by the ego. In reality the ego is like the clown in the circus who gives himself airs to make the audience think that whatever happens is his doing."[13]

Yet during the decade following the letter, unexpectedly and surprisingly Freud's research brought into view an ego that had a significant voice in the fate of the drives. The prankish clown became overseer. After Freud's death the ego even grew into a structure that exerted complete control. That new ego ultimately came to be a self-important, presumptuous, self-infatuated, pompous fellow that knew everything and could achieve every reasonable goal it set up. It prided itself on holding the inner forces at bay, on using the drives for its own purposes, and on ruling over external forces as well. There was no limit to its ability to gain insight into reality and adjust to it. It integrated its society's values and lived in

[13]Ralph Manheim (McGuire, 1974, p. 400) translated Freud's saying of the clown, *seinen Kren dazu geben* (literally, "to add his horseradish") with "to put in his oar."

accordance with them. It anticipated the dangers the surroundings harbored and prepared to meet them at an instant's notice.

To the ego's putative ability to cope with intrapersonal as well as extraneous dangers, I find a counterpart in what happened all around it, the staggering rise of technology that has made man the master of nature. Man has become immune even to erstwhile disastrous sicknesses, and there is no end to the things that can be produced by the use of substances that only man dreamed of: nature lay at his feet ready to be exploited again and again. Technology has become limitlessly powerful, and with it man's ego, as it is made out in the recent turn of psychoanalysis. Even the death drive, which was introduced by Freud as covertly nibbling at man's vitality, is diverted toward reality. In alliance with libido the ego converts this most dangerous fiend into activity, rivalry and mastery, which stand the ego in good stead in attaining its multifarious purposes.

There is only one moment in which, despite technology's great success in prolonging individual life, it has nevertheless failed man. Oddly enough, that is the moment of the drive's ultimate triumph. When the guillotine decapitates the wise and the foolish, the rich and the poor, the beautiful and the ugly, the death drive finds its fullest gratification. And yet it is a Pyrrhic victory, the drive spitting in its own face, like a clown in the circus who would flatter himself to be master over all until he collapses into himself.

Prior to Freud the drives were safely wrapped up by the superego and its representatives, which tyrannized them with the power of religion, churches, and feudalism. To be sure, the Crusades, the burning of dissidents, offered wholesome discharge of drives, but they had to ask for permission, needing the Lord's franchise before they could proceed. Revolutions and other upheavals of the nineteenth century changed the social scenery and lifted some of the reins under which the drives had to smart. Freud's work reflected the forces that had fought at the barricades for the sake of freedom. A distant echo from the barricades may be felt in Freud's epigraph to his dream book *Flectere si nequeo superos, Acheronta movebo* (If I cannot bend the higher powers, I will move the Infernal Regions [from Virgil's *Aeneid*]; Freud, 1900, p. ix). Yet in a letter of 1927 he denied any Promethean or Titanic quality one might easily have read into it but maintained that his using that verse as an epigraph had no other but a psychological meaning for him (Freud, 1960, p. 375).

Whether I interpreted Freud's development accurately or not, it is as true that Freud was correct in saying in his history of the movement (1914, p. 21) that he was one of those "who had disturbed the sleep of the world" (he had done so lastingly and intrusively) as it is true that in recent decades no writing has reached the world from within the boundaries of psychoanalysis that would have had the power of disturbing the sleep of the world. The appearance of satiation, of satisfaction with self, the lack of stirring conflicts, of any revolutionary swing, of any turn against the world as it is, those are some of the unpleasant features that a few analysts believe they perceive in today's psychoanalytic ego and occasionally criticize. The reality which that putative ego is made to deal with is not reality as it is, in which many an irony lurks, eventually outwitting the ego.

They are multiform, rarely humorous, more often tragic; they fill private lives.

My late friend Paul Kramer cured a young woman of her flying phobia. Years later she perished with her husband in a plane accident.

But immeasurably tragic irony reigns on the stage of world history as well. The elite at the top, in each instance, believe themselves to be in control, are optimistic and sure of themselves. Their deeds are aimed at eternity, addressing the welfare of their nation and, if possible, that of mankind. To a certain extent their bearing is reminiscent of the psychoanalytic ego after it has risen from the couch. The top is not aware that its days are counted and its downfall impending. The powerful topple. Empires succeed empires. Where is Caesar's Rome, the Spanish Empire, the British, the German, the Japanese, the Russian? All have been swept away, and one wonders whether this "toppling" ends in an empire that is luxuriously equipped with nuclear power, has stealth bombers that can destroy any building, wherever it may be located, and is invincible. Will that empire be subjected to the rule of history, or can power at last make itself continuous in one historical entity? Empires until now have followed the iron rule of organisms: birth, growth, and collapse—Spengler's view of history has proved correct so far. The irony of history is not likely to have come to an end.

Is that irony of final collapse despite greatest feats of organization—as realized perhaps most magnificently in the Roman Empire—a sumptuous banquet of the untamed drive of self-destruction, outwitting again the ego that believes itself to be clever and ingenious when it is only crafty and cunning, when looked at through the historical eyeglass? The careful exploration of those ironies that outwit the ego is fascinating. They are a warning that the trees do not grow into the sky, as the story of the tower of Babel vainly transmitted. I pride myself on having discovered one of those less conspicuous paths irony takes in tricking the ego by slander.

In earlier times, when a person left his home in the morning he was not certain whether he would not return full of smallpox's deadly toxin. Today smallpox exists only in laboratories and is safely locked up. Vaccination has become superfluous. But today, when a person leaves his home, he is uncertain whether he will not return poisoned by a stigma that slander has fastened on him for good, and there will never be a vaccine against slander.

* * * * *

One will find fault with what looks more like a historical fantasy than serious exploration. Be that as it may, it is high time to return to the subject matter and emphasize how distressing it is to notice that from the portals of academic institutions that are regarded as citadels of propriety, disregard of truth reaches the general reader. There should be a salubrious distance between the vulgarity of the tabloid and academia.

In order to end on a friendlier note, I quote a passage allegedly coming from Leonardo da Vinci, to which Emanuel E. Garcia was kind enough to draw my attention.

> The judgment of an enemy is not infrequently of more truth and benefit than the judgment of a friend.

Hatred in men is almost always deeper than love. The gaze of one who hates is more penetrating than the gaze of one who loves. A true friend is like to thyself. An enemy does not resemble thee,—therein is his strength. Hatred illumines much that is hidden from love. Remember this, and do not contemn the censure of enemies [Merejkowski, 1928, p. 166].

REFERENCES

Bassen, C. R. (1988), The impact of the analyst's pregnancy on the course of analysis. *Psychoanalytic Inquiry*, 8:280–298.

Eissler, K. R. (1955), *The Psychiatrist and the Dying Patient*. New York: International Universities Press.

——— (1972), To Muriel Gardiner on her 70th birthday. *Bull. Philadelphia Assoc. Psychoanal.*, 22:110–130.

Freud, S. (1871), Zerstreute Gedanken. In: K. R. Eissler (et al.), Aus Freuds Sprachwelt und andere Beiträge. *Jahrbuch der Psychoanalyse*, 1974, Beiheft, 2:101.

——— (1900), The Interpretation of Dreams. *Standard Edition*, 5. London: Hogarth Press, 1953.

——— (1905), Fragment of an analysis of a case of hysteria. *Standard Edition*, 7:3–122. London: Hogarth Press, 1953.

——— (1910), The future prospects of psycho-analytic therapy. *Standard Edition*, 11:141–151. London: Hogarth Press, 1957.

——— (1914), On the history of the psycho-analytic movement. *Standard Edition*, 14:3–66. London: Hogarth Press, 1957.

——— (1915), Observations on transference love. *Standard Edition*, 12:159–171. London: Hogarth Press, 1958.

——— (1937), Analysis terminable and interminable. *Standard Edition*, 23:216–253. London: Hogarth Press, 1964.

——— (1960), *Letters of Sigmund Freud*, ed. Ernest L. Freud, trans. Tania and James Stern. New York: Basic Books.

Gay, P. (1988), *Freud: A Life for Our Time*. New York: Norton

Hoffer, A. (1989), Letter to the editor. *New York Review of Books*, 36, No. 13, p. 60f.

Jones, E. (1957), *The Life and Work of Sigmund Freud*, vol. 3. New York: Basic Books.

Jung, C. G. (1910), Ein Beitrag zur Psychologie des Gerüchtes. *Zentralblatt der Psychoanalyse*, 1:81–90.

McGuire, W., ed. (1974), *The Freud/Jung Letters*, trans. Ralph Manheim and R. F. C. Hull. Princeton, NJ: Princeton University Press (Bollingen Series XCIV).

Menaker, E. (1989), *Encounter in Vienna*. New York: St. Martin's Press.

Merejkowski, D. (1928), *The Romance of Leonardo da Vinci*, trans. B. G. Guerney. New York: Modern Library.

Schreber, D. P. (1903), *Memoirs of My Nervous Illness*, trans. I. Macalpine and R. A. Hunter. London: William Dawson, 1955.

Schur, M. (1972), *Freud Living and Dying*. New York: International Universities Press.

Selmi, P. M., Klein, M. H., Greist, J. H., Sorrell, S. P., & Erdman, H. P. (1990), Computer-administered cognitive behavioral therapy for Depression. *A. J. Psychiatry*, 147:1, January 1990.

Woolf, L. (1967), *Downhill All the Way: An Autobiography of the Years 1919-1939*. New York: Harcourt Brace Jovanovich.

Young-Bruehl, E. (1988), *Anna Freud: A Biography*. New York: Summit Books.

EPILOGUE

Philosophers have speculated about justice extensively without discovering a framework of ideas on which the righteous could walk securely. I believe a satisfactory definition of justice has not been established and probably never will be. Moreover, surprisingly little has been heard from the philosophers about injustice, although justice, at least as it is grasped when common sense or intuition is used, is rarely encountered whereas injustice is rampant. This probably happens by virtue of the interest aroused in the more comprehensive subjects of evil and sin, in which injustice holds an only subordinate place.

Wherever one looks, one perceives injustice. A poetic mind that lends sentient qualities to the universe will not derive the consolation from the stars that Kant did but will feel stressed by the disorder he hears about, and will regret the injustice that some ancient stars go on shining brilliantly while their contemporaries have collapsed into black holes. The injustice encountered in the skies extends to nature in a sinister way: spirited animals endowed with brains and sensitivity are devoured alive. No theologian has tackled the enigma of how to reconcile the divinity's selection of one animal for another's meal with considerations of fairness. Until that conundrum is solved, one cannot but hope that the supreme being will finally purge itself of inequities.

The human world, too, teems with injustice and rivals cosmos and nature: infants born crippled, adults disfigured and handicapped by neglect and misfortune that have occurred during their development. Nature has been unmercifully cruel—before the advent of modern medicine, and even since then, many have had to pay a heavy price for survival. Even in sacred texts, where one would least have expected to find it, one encounters injustice profusely, as exemplified in the Lord's forcing Pharaoh, against his will, to deny the Israelites their exodus but nevertheless killing all first-born sons for retribution. Still worse, the taint of original sin, as many are convinced, is transmitted upon conception. A fetus who dies in the womb or a still-born infant therefore must spend eternity in limbo, a kind of hell. This would mean that a being created in the image of God would be condemned to eternal suffering because an ancestor numberless years earlier had disobeyed his creator on a single occasion.

Philosophers argue about which injustice is graver, that of nature or that of society, which places grossly excessive wealth into the hands of a few, reserving to the vast masses the states of poverty-stricken onlookers. But without any exception based on economic or social status, mankind has had to bow to pestilence, famine, earthquakes, floods. Man is threatened from all sides, and only a few reach their last days in the satiety of the Biblical patriarchs. Struggle as man may, stick to the path of virtue as closely as he can, his goodness will not be rewarded and injustice's cold hand is sure to grab him, were it only in the form of inescapable death. Meekness is promised its guerdon in Heaven, but man increasingly prefers the certainty of secular felicity during the life below to the uncertainty of heavenly beneficence. Man has been deceived too often by illusion.

In the psychoanalytic situation it is noteworthy that although each individual vociferously resents being the prey of injustice, one discovers in many, if not all, upon deeper exploration, a profound feeling of guilt and consequent need for expiation; the injustices of which the patient complains then appear to have been deserved punishments. The unravelling of what the past misdeeds were or might have been belongs to the hardest tasks of psychotherapy.

One may also single out the injustice of the historical process. The victims of the Inquisition, the Crusades, of unending wars, of Hiroshima, Nagasaki, the Holocaust suffered macabre injustices whose egregiousness is usually toned down in the course of time and gradually forgotten.

Nature, society, culture, governments—all share responsibility for injustice. In my three essays I have nowhere, except when commenting on capital punishment and death row, even come close to any of these sources.

The second essay deals with the deception that was spread years ago regarding a great mind, Freud, who for the last three or four decades has been the butt of frequent slander. Here would have been a suitable occasion to comment upon that continuous process of maligning. But I am as puzzled as many others as to its causes. The fact that C. G. Jung's was the source of the deception I discussed may arouse interest because it would not have been expected of him. Jung's story concerned Freud's sex life. Since relatively little is known about that topic in relation to geniuses, my proof that Jung's tale of Freud's relationship with his sister-in-law was erroneous may be more important than it may seem.

In the last essay I tried to come closer to a vexing problem of psychoanalytic technique that is of interest since, as I believe, no adequate method of meeting it is at hand. The topic of detraction of the therapist and its possible consequences favored an extension of discussion to include the general problem of misrepresentation, which plays such a prominent role in group life. What is really the source of man's secret hankering to observe his fellowman's defects? I have not pursued that challenging problem to its bitter end, but was finally inclined to discern a positive, though occult, element in slander. In so doing, I followed an anfractuous path, for which I have to apologize. But phenomena look quite different from close up and afar. Both views sometimes have to be presented and this may result in contradictions.

Injustice is unavoidable and will persist as long as society exists. I presented some examples of the underbrush, of the small pinpricks that sustain it.

Do these pinpricks compose the foundation of the great calamities mankind has to endure? At the bottom of fatal diseases one discovers germs and infusoria invisible to the naked eye. With their elimination the storm that fells the strongest ceases. Would the same happen to the great calamities if the underbrush were extinguished, if parents were to let their progeny grow up by imposing on them only the minimum interference, if schools, courts, society at large acted optimally for the common welfare? The degree to which practice can come close to an environment of that near perfection is guesswork, but the probability that it ever will is minimal.

Whether the foregoing three essays have much value beyond their telling a story is not for me to decide. The least that can be said is that they confirm Freud's views about human nature which were quite pessimistic at times.

ACKNOWLEDGMENTS

I would like to thank Michael Meyer for editing the manuscript; William McGuire for correcting inaccuracies in the second essay; S. Clifford B. Yorke, F.R.C.Psych., D.P.M., for an improvement in the third essay; Lawrence M. Siegel, D. Min., for bibliographical references; Carol Kleinman, M.D., for permission to reproduce a letter of hers. Marion Palmedo typed the manuscript and improved it on frequent occasions. Stefanie Kiceluk, Ph.D., solved a treacherous literary problem with her inimitable editorial skills. Finally, I am obliged to Margaret Emery, Ph.D., for accepting the manuscript and graciously publishing it with barely a change.

Name Index

Abraham, K., 143
Adler, A., 110, 143, 241
Aichhorn, A., 103
Alan of Lille, 162n
Aquinas, T., 55, 76
Aristophanes, 66–67
Aristotle, 101
Augustine, St., 56n

Barnhart, E. D., 70
Bassen, C. R., 192
Bedau, H. A., 74
Benedek, E. P., 17, 42, 44–48, 96, 102
Bennet, E. A., 110–111, 131n
Bernays, Martha, 108
Bernays, Minna, 108–110, 121–122, 124, 127–128, 141, 178–180
Billinsky, J. M., 109–117, 119, 121, 125–131, 142, 144–145, 177–180
Binswanger, L., 176
Blackmun, H., 86
Bleuler, E., 165, 169
Brandley, C. L., 76–80
Brennan, W., 73–74
Breuer, J., 145
Bush, G., 60n, 67, 68–71

Carotenuto, A., 124, 137, 142, 144, 173
Chaplin, C., 28
Chin, P., 99
Choisy, M., 126
Collins, L., 75
Corvin, D., 13, 18
Cremerius, 142

da Vinci, L., 213, 245–246
Dante, 206
Darden, W., 86
Davies, N., 76–80
de Angelis, C., 12
Dixon, H. B., Jr., 1–2, 8, 9–10, 11, 15–16, 25–42, 46, 52–53, 91–105
Dostoevsky, F., 43, 76
Duncan, M. G., 72
Dworkin, R., 87–88

Eissler, K. R., 107n, 127n, 202–203, 227–228
Ellenberger, H., 157, 158
Epstein, J. G., 83
Erdman, H. P., 189

Ferenczi, S., 204, 206, 207, 214

257

Fergeson, C., 76
Fichtner, G., 212–213
Finnis, J., 54–55, 61
Fliess, W., 145–146, 178
Foretich, E., 1–53, 91–105
Foretich, H., 1–49, 93–105
Foretich, S., 3–5, 8
Fremont, C., 99
Fretta, N., 18
Freud, A., 94, 178n, 193, 203, 204, 210–212, 217, 230–232, 236
Freud, E., 119n, 178n
Freud, Martha, 120–121, 122–123, 176, 179–180
Freud, Martin, 118n, 119–120
Freud, S., 108–111, 112–182, 185, 188n, 189n, 192, 193, 197, 202–216, 219, 241–244, 251–252, 253
Froning, M., 13, 24, 26
Fujimor, A., 64–65

Garcia, E. E., 245–246
Gardiner, M., 219–221
Gay, P., 108, 127n, 178n, 201, 202–209, 211–216, 219, 221–222, 227–230, 235–236, 238–239
Goethe, 33, 157
Goldstein, J., 94
Green, A., 17
Greist, J. H., 189
Groesbeck, C. J., 125n

Hall, G. S., 110
Hand, L., 237
Harrison, D., 12–13
Hill, A., 66n
Hirschmüller, A., 178n
Hitler, A., 52

Hoffer, A., 204
Holman, L., 15, 97
Honegger, J. J., 125n
Hull, R. F. C., 117, 127, 131, 177

Ingle, J. B., 73–74, 86

Jones, E., 109, 110n, 119n, 192, 204, 214
Jung, C. G., 107–182, 189n, 199–200, 241, 251–252
Jung, E., 114, 173–174, 175

Kafka, F., 83
Kant, I., 249
Killea, L., 63–64
Klein, M. H., 189
Kleinman, C., 18, 47, 102
Kramer, L., 99
Kramer, P., 244
Kranefeldt, M., 143–144

Lewis, A., 70–71, 80–81, 84–85

Mahler, L. T., 63, 64
Manheim, R., 241n
Martin, J., 77–78
Marx, K., 179
Masson, J. M., 181–182, 236n
McGuire, W., 112n, 115, 117, 127, 131, 173, 174n, 177, 189n, 241n
Meier, C. A., 111
Menaker, E., 229–230, 235
Merejkowski, D., 245–246
Michel, P., 97–98
Monroe, R., 74–76
Morgan, E., 1–53, 91–105
Morgan, W., 11
Morrison-Gilstrap, D., 7–8, 9, 18

Moultrie, C., 25
Mumford, L., 179

Newton, I., 40
Nixon, R., 68
Noshpitz, J., 7, 17

Ostow, M., 143–144

Parin, P., 232–234
Pfister, O., 203
Pickett, P., 77–80
Plato, 73, 235
Posner, R. A., 59, 61
Putnam, F., 14

Radelet, M. L., 74
Ranke-Heinemann, U., 55n
Reagan, R., 25, 68, 71
Rehnquist, W., 82–88
Roazen, P., 236n
Rollinson, B. C., 14
Rosenfeld, E., 108–109, 192

Savage, P., 15
Schönberg, I., 108
Schreber, D. P., 206–208
Schur, M., 193
Selmi, P. M., 189

Shubin, C., 12
Simon, K., 57
Sims Podesta, J., 99
Solms, 210–211
Solnit, A., 94
Sophocles, 107
Sorrell, S. P., 189
Spielrein, S., 124, 136–137, 139–142,
    144, 171, 173, 175
Stargardt, J. A., 143–144

Ten Broek, J., 70
Thompson, J., 54, 61

van den Haag, E., 74
Virgil, 206, 243
von Stein, 33

Watson, F. W., 70
Williams, R., 11, 29
Williams, S., 16
Wolff, A., 171–175, 180
Woolf, L., 213

Young-Bruehl, E., 201, 204, 209–213,
    216–217, 227–231, 235–236,
    238–239

Zuckerman, W., 18

SUBJECT INDEX

Abortion issue, 51–52, 53–67
  religion in, 57–60
Academic standards, 231–232
Aggrandizement, 153–158
Aggressor, identification with, 195–196
Alcoholism, in therapist, 234–235
Analytic process, effect of denigration of therapist on, 232–237, 252
Anti-choice movement, 54, 61–65
Assault on Truth: Freud's Suppression of the Seduction Theory, 181

Blacks
  on death row, 81–82
  lack of equal justice for, 74–82
Brandley case, 76–82
Bush administration, Supreme Court under, 67–71

Cain, sign of, 69
Capital cases, defense counsel in, 70–71
Capital punishment
  abolishment of, 80–81, 88–90
  arguments supporting, 72–73
  corrosive effect of, on society, 73–74
  delays in, 85–86
  issue of, 71–90
  for mentally retarded and psychotic, 86–88
Catholic Church, on abortion issue, 57–59, 62–65
Child abuser, personality of, 18–22
Child sexual abuse
  case history of, 1–8
  child's welfare and, 39–42, 94–105
  difficulty in establishing truth of, 32–35
  expert testimony in, 12–13, 17–18, 42–49
  gathering evidence of, 8–9
  justified suspicion and conclusive evidence in, 8–49
Child testimony, reliability of, 34–35
Child welfare, legal system and, 39–42, 94–105
Civil rights, Supreme Court and, 82–90
Collective unconscious, 169–170
  flight into, 148, 151–152
Computerized therapy, 188–190
Concentration camps, death row and, 81

Conclusive evidence, 35–49
Confabulation, 142–144, 201, 211–213
Confession, enforced, 82, 85
Constitution
    Article II, Section 2, 92
    Rehnquisition and, 87–88
    violation of, 84–85
Contempt of court, incarceration for, 25
Contraception, as murder, 55–56

Death penalty. *See* Capital punishment
Death row, 71–72
    blacks on, 81–82
Deception, 251–252
Defense counsel, need for standards in, 70–71
Depression, in abused child, 14–15
Doomed world phase, 149–153
Dora case, transference in, 185
Dream analysis
    free association in, 147–148
    Freud's, 125–126, 134–136
Drives, ego and, 241–244
Drug addiction, therapist's, 234–235

Ego
    coping ability of, 241–242
    drives and, 242–244
    subordinate role of, 241
    toppling of, 244–245
Eighth Amendment, 89
Enemy, judgment of, 245–246
Evidence
    admissibility of, 35–36
    conclusive, 27–49
Expert testimony, 94–95

Family planning, Catholic Church

and, 64–65
Father
    conflicts with, 164–165
    preoedipal tie to, 163–164
Feminism, 51
Fliess letters, 211–212
Freud-Bernays relationship, 108–112, 178–180
Freud-Jung split, 110–182
Freud Literary Heritage Foundation, 204
Freud's letters
    in biography, 212–216
    to fiancée, 212
    misreading of, 206–209
    publication of, 202–209
Friends of Elizabeth Morgan, 2

God, Jung's belief in, 170–171
Gossip
    forms of, 194
    object of, 197–198
    patient-therapist relationship and, 217–223
    psychoanalysis of, 199
    soft-core, 196
    against therapist, 194–246
    therapist and, 223–227
    transference and, 217–219, 226–227
    truth value of, 198–199
Gossipers, types of, 200–201
Grandiosity, 153–158
Guilt, 251

Harmless-error rule, 82, 84–85
History, irony of, 244–245
Homosexual conflicts, 164–167
Homosexuality, therapist's, 234–235

Incest. *See also* Child sexual abuse;

Morgan-Foretich case
child's welfare and, 94–105
father-daughter vs. mother-son, 100
Informants, motives of, 231
Injustice
of nature vs. society, 250–251
pervasiveness of, 249–250
responsibility for, 251
Innocent, execution of, 86–88
International Psychoanalytic Association, 27th Congress of, 209–210
International Psychoanalytic Congress in Nuremberg, Second, 166
The Interpretation of Dreams, 145–146
Intolerance, 59–60

Japanese internment, 70
Jung-Spielrein affair, 136–144
Jung-Wolff liaison, 173–175
Justice, philosophical speculation about, 249–250
Justified suspicion/conclusive evidence issue, 7–49

Lysistrata, 66–67

The Making of a Woman Surgeon, 3
McClosky case, 84–86, 89
Memoirs of My Nervous Illness, 206
Memories, Dreams, Reflections, 127, 129, 135, 145–147, 156–157, 169, 176–177, 180
Memories, unreliability of, 107–182
Mentally ill, death penalty for, 86–88
Miranda rule, 82
Morgan-Foretich case

justified suspicion and conclusive evidence in, 1–49
women's rights and, 52–53, 91–105
Motherhood, enforced, 60–61
Multiple personality disorder, 14
Murder-abortion thesis, 55–56

Narcissistic conflicts, 164, 167–169
National Socialist Party (German), 51–52
Nazi Germany, women's rights in, 51–52
Newsletter of Friends of Elizabeth Morgan, 101

Oedipus conflict, 145
Overpopulation, 56–57
anti-choice movement and, 64–65

Paternity cases, evidence in, 28
Patient-therapist relationship, effect of gossip on, 217–223
Philemon figure, 154–156, 169
Pregnancy
enforced, 60–61
women's rights and, 51–52, 53–67
Psychiatric testimony, reliability of, 42–49
Psychoanalytic technique, problem of transference in, 185–246
Psychology of the Unconscious, 117, 146, 152–153
Psychosis, course of, 146–158

Reagan administration, Supreme Court under, 67–70
Reasonable doubt, 39
Regression, 147–149
Rehnquisition, 82–90

Religious authority, 57–60
Reputation
    responsibility for, 238–240
    sources of, 238–239
Resistance, denigration of therapist
        and, 220–221
Restitution phase, 153–158
Retarded, death penalty for, 86–88
Right-to-life movement, 54
    Catholic Church in, 62–65
    coerciveness of, 61–62
Rust v. Sullivan, 88

Seduction theory, suppression of,
        181
Self-aggrandizement, 161
Self-destructiveness, 195–196
Self-image, slander and, 225–226
Septem Sermones ad Mortuos, 156–157,
        164
Sexual abuse, child. *See* Child sexual
        abuse
Sigmund Freud Archives, 202–204
Slander
    background of, 236
    effect of, on therapist, 223–227
    effect on analytic process, 232–237
    outwitting of ego by, 241–245
    roots in deeply repressed, 239–240
    skill of assertion of, 228–231
Slanderer, pathological, 200
Social image, slander and, 223–225
Solomon, wisdom of, 27–32
Son, unconscious death wish
        against, 151–153
Splitting, pathological, 159–161
Suicide, death penalty and, 89
Supreme Court
    on abortion issue, 51–52, 53–67
    on capital punishment and civil

    rights, 71–90
    Morgan-Foretich case and, 91–105
    under Reagan and Bush adminis-
        trations, 68–71
    women's rights and, 50–105
Suspicion
    versus conclusive evidence, 27–49
    doubt and, 100–101

Tabula rasa phase, 146–147
Therapist
    alcoholism, addiction, or homo-
        sexuality of, 234–235
    dehumanization of, 188–189
    elimination of, 189–190
    gossip or rumors about, 194–246
    maligning of, 185–246, 252
    objective realities about, 190–193
    patient's personal knowledge of,
        234–237
    training of, 191–192
"Three Essays on the Theory of Sex-
        uality," 146
Transference
    contamination of, 187–246
    dangers of, 124–125
    discovery of, 185–186
    process of, 186–188
    slander effects on, 226–227
Tua res agitur rule, 226–227
Twilight states, 104

Unconscious, personal versus collec-
        tive, 148, 151–152, 169–170

Victimology, 21–22, 238

Wandlungen, 112–115, 117

White Lies: Rape, Murder, and Justice Texas Style, 76n

Witnesses, unreliability of memory in, 107–182

Women, discrimination against, 50–51

Women's Liberation Movement, 51

Women's rights
abortion issue and, 51–52, 53–67
assault against, 48–49
Morgan-Foretich custody case and, 52–53, 91–105
pro-choice movement and, 65–67
Supreme Court and, 50–105